A Year in the Garden

A Monthly Gardening Guide

for the Gulf South

Published by:
Friends of Magnolia Mound Plantation, Inc.
P. O. Box 45848
Baton Rouge, LA 70895

Printed by:
FRP
2451 Atrium Way
Nashville, TN 37214

Printed in China

Cataloging in Publication Data is Available.

ISBN: 978-0-9798812-0-6

First Printing Edition 2007

Compiled and Edited by: Patricia Comeaux and Jane Thomas

Designed by: Jane Thomas, Thomasgraphics

Book Committee: Jane Thomas, *Chairman*; Patricia Comeaux; Jon Emerson; Debbie Hudson; Mary Lynn McMains; Cheryl Stromeyer

On the cover:

The Magnolia Mound Plantation Kitchen and Garden

Photography Credits:

Gaspar Avila	Lior Filshteiner	Aleksandr Lobanov	William Sarver
Pat Borowicz	Susan Fox	William Mahnken	Babeth Schlegel
Paul Brennan	Lijuan Guo	Mary Lynn McMains	Tom Schmucker
Yriy Brykaylo	Anton Gvozdikov	Chartchai Meesangnin	Colin Stitt
Brian K. Crain	Denise Kappa	Glaina Moiseeva	Jane Thomas
Bob Deneizen	Ewa Kuabicka	Tim Mueller	Robert Young
Elke Dennis	Tamara Kulikova	Anita Patterson Peppers	
Elena Elisseeva	Emilia Kun	Julian Pond	
Engin Communications	Svetlana Larina	Allan Pospisil	

A Year in the Garden

A Monthly Gardening Guide

for the Gulf South

A project of the

Friends of Magnolia Mound Plantation, Inc.

Baton Rouge, Louisiana

Acknowledgements to

the Baton Rouge Landscape Association for providing the gardening information for the first book published in 1989; the Baton Rouge Recreation and Parks Commission of East Baton Rouge Parish for their outstanding stewardship of Magnolia Mound Plantation; the East Baton Rouge Parish Master Gardeners' Association for their loving care of the Kitchen Garden; to historians Winnie Byrd and Gwen Edwards and staff members Susan Moreau, Jenny Poulter and Babeth Schlegel for their assistance with the historical section added to the book; to the LSU Libraries, Hill Memorial Library for their assistance in researching Magnolia Mound and the Duplantier papers in their collections; to Greg Grant and Kenny Kleinpeter for their contributions to the text; to Judy Hotard and Laura Webb for their assistance in proofing the manuscript; to Carolyn Goyer for the final proofing; to Allen Owings with the LSU AgCenter for his enthusiasm and assistance; to the LSU AgCenter as a primary source of information; to Sidney M. Blitzer, Scott N. Hensgens and Emile C. Rolfs, III of Breazeale Sachse and Wilson, Attorneys at Law for their legal assistance; to Steve Yates for his expert marketing advice; to staff members Carey Coxe and Charlene Bertrand and to the Friends of Magnolia Mound Plantation Board of Directors for their strong and continued support of this project.

A Year in the Garden

Growing something in a garden can be one of the most satisfying experiences in life. It is what provides roots and makes a place "home."

This monthly guide has been created to make gardening as pleasurable and successful as possible. Originally designed for Baton Rouge, Louisiana, and surrounding areas, the guide has been expanded to include the Gulf Coast.

Gardening in the South can be a challenge. At times rainfall may almost reach the level of a tropical rainforest and everything washes away. Other times may be plagued with drought and everything will dry out and die. The weather is not consistent from year to year. Vigilance is mandatory and an automatic irrigation system is not as much a luxury as it is peace of mind. Climate zones may squeeze an area into an "almost zone" where plants that are treasured from the north, such as lilacs, peonies and cherries, "almost" grow. However, there is not enough cool weather to satisfy their chilling requirements and the summers are just too hot. Cherished tropicals seldom survive when temperatures dip into the twenties which can happen from time to time even along the Gulf Coast.

Gardening in the Gulf South may take extra work but the results can be spectacular. This guide will demonstrate the astounding number of plants that are grown successfully in the Gulf South every month. The purpose of the guide is to present all of the possibilities for a beautiful garden and a plan of how to reach the goal of each gardener.

The inspiration for this book

came from the sell-out of over 10,000 books, entitled *A Year in the Garden,* a joint project of the Board of Trustees of Magnolia Mound Plantation and the Baton Rouge Landscape Association, first printed in 1989 and now out of print.

After repeated requests from area gardeners for copies, the members of the Friends of Magnolia Mound Plantation began the task of rewriting and redesigning the book, to include not only the original garden information, but also to update and expand the information for gardeners across the Gulf Coast.

A Year in the Garden: A Monthly Gardening Guide for the Gulf South is designed to be user-friendly. Information on what to plant and how to take care of the garden is divided by months.

At the end of each monthly section are lists of what to seed or transplant, what's in bloom, and what to harvest. These lists also correspond to the charts at the end of the garden section.

Articles on recommended roses, azaleas, crape myrtles and fruits are included as well as a sprinkling of historical notes, old recipes, "lagniappe" and many beautiful photographs. The book also includes a section on Magnolia Mound Plantation.

Table of Contents

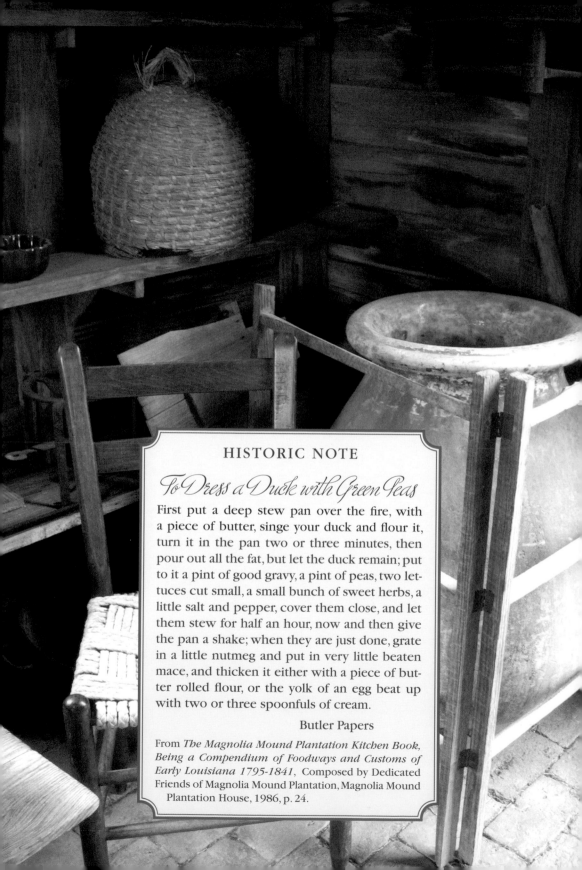

HISTORIC NOTE

To Dress a Duck with Green Peas

First put a deep stew pan over the fire, with a piece of butter, singe your duck and flour it, turn it in the pan two or three minutes, then pour out all the fat, but let the duck remain; put to it a pint of good gravy, a pint of peas, two lettuces cut small, a small bunch of sweet herbs, a little salt and pepper, cover them close, and let them stew for half an hour, now and then give the pan a shake; when they are just done, grate in a little nutmeg and put in very little beaten mace, and thicken it either with a piece of butter rolled flour, or the yolk of an egg beat up with two or three spoonfuls of cream.

Butler Papers

From *The Magnolia Mound Plantation Kitchen Book, Being a Compendium of Foodways and Customs of Early Louisiana 1795-1841*, Composed by Dedicated Friends of Magnolia Mound Plantation, Magnolia Mound Plantation House, 1986, p. 24.

January is the month to dream, to make sketches, to plan flower beds, to order seeds and supplies and to anticipate an entire glorious year in the garden. Begin by taking soil samples for pH and fertility testing. Call a county agent for details. Use this month to repair garden tools, such as weed trimmers, lawn mowers and tillers. Change oil, air filters and spark plugs. Replace worn belts and sharpen blades.

Check the garden chemical shelf and dispose of old bottles of chemicals. In many, the active ingredient will lose potency, and will also break down, causing more harm than the insects. Be sure to dispose of according to label directions and always store chemicals where children and pets can't get to them.

Enjoy the garden in January, for it isn't bare despite the cold wet days. The beautiful blossoms of camellias will make northern friends envious.

CULTURE

Keep annuals blooming longer by dead-heading or removing the spent and faded flowers. It is especially important in lengthening the bloom of pansies but is also beneficial on almost any annual. Start now and continue throughout the season.

Special garden care for this month includes protecting tender vegetation. Water well before hard freezes. Cut spent flowers on blooming bulbs but leave the foliage on those you wish to repeat, such as daffodils and other narcissus, until at least late April. Weed out wild onion and oxalis weeds with a selective herbicide if possible.

A quiet corner in the Magnolia Mound Plantation kitchen displays an antique clay olla, a ladderback chair and bee skep made of coiled straw.

BULBS

Now is the time to put tulip and hyacinth bulbs that have been chilled into the ground. By planting both mid- and late-blooming tulips, you will extend the blooming season. Plant in full shade with one inch of soil covering the top of the bulb. When using bulb fertilizer or cottonseed meal, avoid direct contact with the bulb. Consider color combinations with other blooming plants.

PERENNIALS AND HERBS

This is a good month to check for drainage problems. Winter root rot is the surest way to kill most perennials and herbs. Raise the bed 8 to 12 inches or use plants that tolerate or even prefer "wet feet," such as physostegia, loosestrife, mint and pennyroyal.

ROSES

January is the month to start planting roses. Plant in prepared beds (see November). If weather permits, there is still time to prepare beds. At time of planting prune out crossing, damaged or bruised branches. Prune each stem to an outside bud. This helps in preventing diseases. Space plants 3 or 4 feet apart. Water in with a starter solution high in phosphorus (15-30-15). Mulch ABOVE the graft-union. Sterilize pruners before using them again by dipping them in a 10% bleach solution or alcohol.

TREES AND SHRUBS

Continue to plant trees and shrubs this month. Consider the following native plants:

Small - honeysuckle azalea, red buckeye, cherry-laurel, fringe tree, dogwood, parsley hawthorne, huckleberry, ironwood, wax myrtle, redbud, silverbell, snowbell, sweetleaf and yaupon holly

Medium - river birch, Eastern red cedar, Southern black cherry, winged elm, fringe tree and American holly

Large - green ash, bald cypress, American beech, sweet gum, hackberry, Southern magnolia, red maple, cherrybark oak, cow oak, live oak, Shumard oak, white oak, loblolly pine, tulip poplar, sassafras and sycamore

Purchase fruit varieties recommended when putting in trees this month. See list on page 75.

Lagniappe
Spading or tilling wet soil will do more damage than good. Wait until the soil is dry enough to crumble.

DRYING AND PRESERVING

Press pansies and johnny-jump-ups between newspapers. These are some of the easiest and best flowers to dry. The yellows and blues hold their color the best.

FIRST WEEK

Plant tulip and hyacinth bulbs.

Start lettuce, cauliflower, broccoli and eggplant in greenhouse.

SECOND WEEK

Root fig cuttings.

THIRD WEEK

Prepare rose beds.

Begin planting Irish potatoes.

Plant a tree for Arbor Day.

FOURTH WEEK

Check lawn equipment.

Begin planting gladiolus bulbs.

Plant roses.

Pansies are one of the most popular annuals for cool weather. They are ideal for placing between beds and paths as an edging or as a filler between rocks or stepping stones, but they don't do well in heat and should be removed when warm weather arrives.

See charts in back of book

Bloom
indicates best bloomers

ANNUALS

Alyssum
Calendula*
Pansy*
Flower Cabbage and
 Kale*
Johnny-Jump-Up*

BULBS

Crocus
Narcissus*

PERENNIALS

Gerbera Daisy
Woods Violet

SHRUBS AND TREES

Camellia japonica*
Holly, berries*
Winter Honeysuckle*
Flowering Quince
Sweet Olive

Seed

FLOWERS

start seed in peat pot

Achillea
Alyssum
Begonia
Calendula
Dahlia
Dianthus
Geranium
Native Hibiscus
Impatiens
Lisianthus
Lobelia
Nicotiana
Ornamental Pepper
Petunia
Phlox drummondii,
 annual
Salvia
Torenia
Verbena

VEGETABLES AND HERBS

plant seed in ground

Beet
Cabbage
Carrot
Mustard Greens
English Peas
Snow Peas
Irish Potato, seed
 potatoes
Radish
Shallot
Spinach
Turnip

start seed in peat pot

Broccoli
Cauliflower
Eggplant
Lettuce
Pepper
Parsley
Tomato

Transplant

FLOWERS

Bluebonnet
Foxglove
Hollyhock
Pansy
Garden Poppy
Iceland Poppy
Shirley Poppy
Snapdragon
Sweet Pea
Tulip

Harvest

VEGETABLES AND HERBS

Brussels Sprouts
Cabbage
Carrot
Mustard Greens
Parsley
Radish
Shallot
Spinach
Turnip

Often thought of as tiny cabbages, Brussels sprouts are believed to have originated in Brussels, Belgium. As early as the sixteenth century, they were popular in the Netherlands. Their popularity eventually spread throughout Europe. Sprouts are delicious if they are harvested when small, compact and bright green and cooked until just tender.

HISTORIC NOTE

Remembering the Past at Magnolia Mound

The history of African Americans who lived and worked as slaves at Magnolia Mound Plantation is presented year-round with special events scheduled each February in observance of Black History month. This slave cabin on the grounds of Magnolia Mound Plantation is a reminder of the hardships endured by an enslaved people.

February is the month to prepare perennial flower beds. Make note of the sun patterns in the yard before selecting a site. Choose a sunny location, although many plants prefer some protection from the hot afternoon sun. Mulch new plantings to help keep the soil cooler and to reduce weed competition.

Due to heavy clay soils and high annual rainfall, excellent drainage is the key to a successful garden. Improve the site by raising the bed with landscape timbers or treated lumber. Organic matter and coarse builder's sand may be added to the soil to improve tilth and drainage. When preparing beds, incorporate a complete fertilizer and any suggested soil amendments. This is also the time to fertilize existing beds.

CULTURE

Remember the very long growing season when planning annual and perennial beds for the year. Most annuals will not perform well for more than three or four months so consider two plantings for marigolds, zinnias, celosias and cosmos. Before new growth begins apply the first application of complete fertilizer for perennials. Apply a systemic insecticide to daylilies to control aphids. Cut back ornamental grasses to about 6 inches before new growth resumes. Remove any dead foliage or old flower stalks remaining in the beds. Fertilize and prune all fruits except citrus this month. If there is an unexpected freeze, water foliage well before the sun hits the most tender plants. This may prevent freeze burn.

BULBS

Start planting gladiolus bulbs in mid-month, then plant weekly until the middle of March. This will extend their blooming period. Plant them in a sunny area about 3/4 inch deep and about 6 inches apart. Stake the plants to ensure straight flower stems.

ROSES

Begin a preventative spray program alternating fungicides for blackspot and powdery mildew. As foliage emerges, apply a miticide/insecticide to reduce damage. Valentine's Day is an easy date to remember to prune bush-type roses. Prune vigorous plants to a height of 12 to 18 inches. Prune higher if less vigorous. Cut at a 45 degree angle 1/4 inch above an outward bud. Leave 5 to 10 healthy canes per bush. Miniatures should be pruned 1/2 their size before the buds swell. Prune hybrid climbers while dormant. Prune ramblers and vigorous climbers such as Lady Banksia soon after flowering. Canes on climbers are good for two to three seasons and then should be removed to allow new growth. Dip pruners in alcohol or a 10% bleach solution to avoid spreading canker dieback. Fertilizing after pruning will assure large, beautiful blossoms with strong stems.

There are many commercial rose foods. A home mix that we recommend is 1/4 ounce of a complete fertilizer (8-8-8 or 13-13-13), a handful of cottonseed or alfalfa meal, and a handful of magnesium sulfate (Epsom salt) per plant. Work lightly into the soil and water in.

See page 74 for recommended roses.

GROUNDCOVER

This is the time to cut your liriope, monkey grass and Asian jasmine before the new growth emerges. Use a weed trimmer, hedge shears or a lawn mower set very high. Trim to about 4 inches.

LAWNS

Follow label warnings and apply a selective lawn herbicide for weed control. This will weed out wild onions, oxalis, stachys and clovers.

TREES AND SHRUBS

The Taiwan cherry is the first tree to bloom. They bloom so early that they are caught by frost in some years. Fertilize trees and shrubs, using the following formulas:

Trees - Deep-root feed larger specimens with a balanced fertilizer. Use 1 to 2 pounds per year of age. Make holes 12 inches deep beginning 2 feet from the trunk. Fill halfway with fertilizer and cover remainder with sand. Continue circling the tree with holes to the outer edges of the branches (drip line) until all fertilizer is used.

Shrubs - Use 1/4 pound of a complete fertilizer per square yard.

From November through February, prune evergreens and summer and fall flowering shrubs. Spring flowering shrubs should only be pruned after the blooming season. This includes azalea, hydrangea and spirea. When planting trees and shrubs use native soil for backfill. Using excessive amounts of organic matter or sand will promote poor root establishment. Work systemic insecticide into the soil under insect-prone plants such as camellia, gardenia and crape myrtle.

VEGETABLES

Prepare the garden for spring planting. Contact a county agent and request a copy of a vegetable planting guide. Care for your strawberry plants by controlling leaf spot or rust with fungicide until blossoms form. Control spider mites with a miticide recommended for fruits and vegetables. When seeding corn always plant at least 4 rows to allow cross-pollinations by the wind. Early planted corn will have fewer problems with corn earworms.

FIRST WEEK

Plant tulip and hyacinth bulbs.

Start lettuce, cauliflower, broccoli and eggplant in greenhouse.

SECOND WEEK

Prune roses on Valentine's Day or soon after.

Apply a lawn herbicide to prevent weeds.

THIRD WEEK

Plant nasturtium and sweet pea seeds.

Finish pruning evergreens and summer blooming shrubs (not hydrangeas).

FOURTH WEEK

Fertilize all fruit trees, blueberries and blackberries.

Lagniappe

Branches of plum, redbud, flowering quince, forsythia, peach and crabapple can be forced inside. Do not try to force in warm water or the flowers will open irregularly instead of all at once. Change the water frequently.

See charts in back of book

Bloom

* indicates best bloomers

ANNUALS

Alyssum
Calendula*
Flowering Cabbage
  and Kale*
English Daisy
Dianthus
Johnny-Jump-Up*
Lobelia
Pansy*
Petunia
Iceland Poppy

BULBS

Anemone
Crocus
Daffodil*
Hyacinth*
Narcissus
Snowdrops
Tulip*

PERENNIALS

Gerbera Daisy
Woods Violet

TREES AND SHRUBS

Abutilon
"Red Ruffles" Azalea
Camellia japonica*
Taiwan Cherry*
Forsythia
Winter Honeysuckle
Carolina Jasmine
Japanese Magnolia*
Flowering Quince*
Redbud*
Sweet Olive

Seed

FLOWERS

plant seed in ground

Nasturtium
Sweet Pea

FLOWERS

start seed in peat pot

Ageratum
Abelmoschus
Alyssum
Calendula
Coleus
Cosmos
Craspedia
Begonia
Geranium
Hare's Tail Grass
Native Hibiscus
Impatiens
Larkspur
Lisianthus
Marigold
Nicotiana
Pennisetum
Ornamental Pepper
Periwinkle
Petunia
Phlox drummondii,
  annual
Rudbeckia
Salvia
Strawflower
Torenia
Veronica
Xeranthemum
Zinnia

VEGETABLES AND HERBS

plant seed in ground, mid-February

Bush Snap Bean
Carrot
Sweet Corn
Lettuce
Mustard Greens
Parsley
Radish
Shallots
Spinach
Irish Potato, seed
  potatoes

VEGETABLES AND HERBS

start seed in peat pot

Basil
Broccoli
Cauliflower
Dill
Eggplant
Lettuce
Tomato

Transplant

FLOWERS

Dahlia
Dianthus
Gladiolus

VEGETABLES AND HERBS

Mid-February

Broccoli
Lettuce
Peas

Harvest

VEGETABLES AND HERBS

Anise
Cabbage
Carrot
Chervil
Collard
Endive
Fennel
Leek
Mustard
Parsley
Radish
Shallot
Spinach

The camellia, originally from Asia, is an superb evergreen plant and brightens up the winter landscape with its lovely blossoms. Camellias have few disease and insect problems except for tea scale which can be treated with an oil spray.

HISTORIC NOTE

A French Cake Receipt

Take five common-sized tumblers full of sifted flour, three tumblers of powdered white sugar, half a tumbler of butter, one tumbler of rich milk or cream, and a tea-spoonful of pearl ash dissolved in as much lukewarm water as to cover it. Mix all well together in a pan. Beat 3 eggs 'til very light and then add them to the mixture. Throw in a tea-spoonful of powdered cinnamon or nutmeg and beat the whole very hard about 10 min. Butter a deep pan, put in the mixture and bake in a moderate oven.

Baton Rouge Gazette

From *The Magnolia Mound Plantation Kitchen Book, Being a Compendium of Foodways and Customs of Early Louisiana 1795-1841,* Composed by Dedicated Friends of Magnolia Mound Plantation, Magnolia Mound Plantation House, 1986, p.50.

*M*arch is one of the most exciting times in the garden and also one of the busiest. Azaleas make the area glow with color, while dogwood, redbud and flowering pear trees literally burst into bloom. Many perennials and annuals are available now in garden centers. This is the time to fill in those bare spots. Some summer annuals that perform well through fall are caladium, impatiens, begonia, periwinkle and purslane. Use this chart to determine how many plants are needed:

Number of Plants Needed to Cover 100 Sq. Ft.	Inches Between Plants Are
900	4
400	6
225	8
144	10
100	12
64	15
45	18
25	24

CULTURE

Now that the weather is warming up, be on the lookout for insects. If the leaf color looks unusual, turn the leaf over and check the back for spider mites or white flies. Spider mites are tiny and barely visible to the eye. To test if the "dust" on the leaves is spider mites, flick the leaf over a white sheet of paper. If the specks move, it is spider mites. White flies are tiny winged insects also found on the underside of leaves. When the plant is shaken they swarm like a small white cloud. Other insects to look for are aphids, small insects about the size of an "o." When you find one, you find hundreds. They usually congregate on the softest, newest growth of the plant.

It is a good time to dig and divide chrysanthemums. Also divide summer and fall flowering perennials as new growth starts.

PERENNIALS AND HERBS

This is an excellent month to plant an herb garden. Follow the usual recommendations for perennials. Drainage is the most important factor. A whiskey barrel or other large container makes an excellent herb garden. Use good potting soil and mix in a slow-release fertilizer. Make sure the location is in full sun. Water frequently and every two weeks use a water soluble fertilizer.

Annual herbs frequently used are: basil, borage, cilantro, chamomile, chervil, dill, mint marigold, sage and sweet marjoram. Perennial herbs are listed in September.

Most perennials come back so don't be too quick to replant bare areas. Some plants like the native hibiscus, cupheas and liatris emerge later in early to mid-April.

ROSES

Some early roses will be in bud. Continue a preventive spray program. Treat every week either in early morning or late afternoon. It is best to alternate chemicals to prevent resistance. To lessen a chance of foliage burn, spray early in the day. Insects to watch for are spider mites, aphids, thrips and cucumber beetles. Possible diseases are black spot, powdery mildew and stem canker.

Don't push newly planted roses with excessive fertilizer. Applying a liquid solution of 15-30-15 once a month should be sufficient for the next six months. If over fertilized with nitrogen, the top will outgrow the roots and the plant will suffer when the heat sets in. Remember to remove the spent flowers so the plant's energy can go into making more blooms.

TREES AND SHRUBS

This is the month to apply dormant oil to camellias, gardenias and citrus to control scale, whitefly and other sucking insects. Check shrubbery beds to make sure they are well mulched. Apply a pre-emergent herbicide to beds you don't plan to direct seed. Get ready to battle the stinging or buck moth caterpillars in oaks and sweet gums. Also spray peach, plum and nectarine trees to control the plum curculio beetle. Spray just before and after full bloom. Check for fireblight on edible pears. The tips of the branches wilt. Spray when in full bloom. Fireblight can also attack loquat, pyracantha, apple and flowering quince. If you have trees and shrubs you still want to plant, get them in before the heat sets in.

VEGETABLES

Ready the vegetable garden this month. Add mulch and fertilize. Vegetable rows should run north-south with the taller plants on the north end.

FIRST WEEK

Begin your rose spray program.

Prune Asian jasmine.

SECOND WEEK

Make your first mowing at a low setting and remove the clippings.

Finish planting gladiolus bulbs.

Start your herbs early before hot weather.

THIRD WEEK

Plant warm season vegetables, including tomatoes.

Set out hummingbird feeders.

Write the purchase date on pesticide bottles. Dispose of properly after 1 to 2 years.

FOURTH WEEK

Bring a bit of spring into the house with fresh cut flowers from the garden.

Lagniappe

Move houseplants outside. Start them in a shady location. Those that can tolerate it can be gradually moved into more and more sun. Feed with a water soluble fertilizer on a weekly basis.

It is best to use smaller hummingbird feeders. A large feeder filled with sugar water may sour before it is emptied.

To prepare the nectar mix 1 cup of water to 1/4 cup sugar. Heat the mixture to dissolve the sugar if necessary. This may be stored in the refrigerator.

It may take a few weeks initially for the birds to start feeding. A garden containing red blooms may help to attract hummingbirds. Watching hummingbirds feed in a garden is a delightful experience.

See charts in back of book

***indicates best bloomers**

ANNUALS

Alyssum
Bachelor Button
Bluebonnet
Calendula
Dianthus*
English Daisy
Forget-Me-Not
Foxglove*
Geranium*
Johnny-Jump-Up
Lobelia
Nasturtium
Pansy*
Petunia*
Phlox drummondii, annual
Garden Poppy
Shirley Poppy
Queen Anne's Lace
Snapdragon*
Statice
Sweet Pea
Sweet William*
Verbena

BULBS

Amaryllis
Anemone*
Bluebells
Calla Lily
Hyacinth
German Iris, white
Siberian Iris
Yellow Iris
Narcissus
Muscari
Ranunculus, mid-March
Tulip

PERENNIALS

Coreopsis
Gaillardia

Gerbera Daisy
Louisiana Phlox*
Stokesia
Verbena

VINES

Carolina Jasmine*
Primrose Jasmine
Wisteria*

TREES AND SHRUBS

Azalea*
Camellia Japonica
Dogwood*
Forsythia*
Indian Hawthorne*
Pear
Flowering Quince
Redbud
Spirea

Seed

FLOWERS

start seed in peat pot

Abelmoschus
Ageratum
Amaranth
Celosia
Cosmos
Gaillardia
Globe Amaranth
Native Hibiscus
Marigold
Periwinkle
Rudbeckia
Thunbergia
Zinnia

VEGETABLES AND HERBS

plant seed in ground, mid-March

Basil
Beans
Cantaloupe
Cilantro
Corn
Cucumber
Dill

Lettuce
Okra
Southern Peas
Pepper
Pumpkin
Squash
Watermelon

Transplant

Abelmoschus
Ageratum
Alyssum
Begonia
Blue daze
Coleus
Cuphea
Dwarf Dahlia
Dusty Miller
Echinacea
Gaillardia
Geranium
Gerbera Daisy
Gladiolus
Impatiens
Lisianthus
Lobelia
Marigold
Mexican Heather
Nicotiana
Ornamental Pepper
Periwinkle
Louisiana Phlox
Summer Phlox
Rudbeckia
Salvia
Torenia

Verbena
Zinnia

VEGETABLES AND HERBS

Basil
Beans
Cantaloupe
Chives
Cucumber
Eggplant
Lemon Grass
Lettuce
Peppers
Irish potato
Rosemary
Thyme
Tomato

Harvest

VEGETABLES AND HERBS

Carrot
Collard
Leek
Lettuce
Onion
Mustard
Parsley
Peas, late March
Radish
Shallot
Spinach
Turnip

Wisteria adds grace, soft color and scent to a garden.

HISTORIC NOTE

Glace à la Vanille

Crush a demi-gros of vanilla beans. Bring beans and eight ounces of sugar to a boil in half pint of milk, pour it through a filter and freeze it.

Tante Huppe

From *The Magnolia Mound Plantation Kitchen Book, Being a Compendium of Foodways and Customs of Early Louisiana 1795-1841*, Composed by Dedicated Friends of Magnolia Mound Plantation, Magnolia Mound Plantation House, 1986, p. 52.

April remains a riot of color. The number of plants in bloom is staggering and now's a good chance to view the garden as a whole. Experiment and rearrange parts of the garden. Keep flower heights, colors and foliage textures in mind. Place the tall plants towards the back. Pale colors soften and make an area appear to recede. Bright colors focus attention. Bold foliage, like ginger and aspidistra, looks best if contrasted with fine-textured foliage such as ferns.

CULTURE

While enjoying April's beauty, take a few precautions to avoid problems later. Water new plantings and transplants thoroughly. Protect small flowering plants with snail and slug bait. Check plants for spider mites, aphids and caterpillars.

Begin control of leaf roller on canna lily.

Lichens are the fluffy, moss-like growth that appears on some plants, such as crape myrtles. This growth may indicate a non-vigorous plant so look for causes like weed trimmer damage. Lichens are not parasites and do not hurt the plant. Many people enjoy their addition to the garden or they can be controlled with a fixed-copper fungicide.

Spider mites cannot be controlled by all insecticides. Be sure that the label specifically says "miticide." Try to use a systemic chemical as this will minimize the number of sprays needed. Three sprayings 7 to 10 days apart is a good rule.

Do not cut foliage of spring bulbs until it starts turning yellow or the food needed for next year's flowers will be lost.

Perennials will require a second application of fertilizer this month. Make sure the fertilizer does not burn the foliage or the crown of the plant. Water well.

Stake gladiolus and dahlias for straight stalks. Pinch off dead chrysanthemum blossoms every 2 to 3 weeks until mid-July to have shorter, fuller plants covered in blossoms. Divide after they finish blooming.

Plant caladiums 1/2 to 1 inch deep and continue through May. Earlier plantings may rot before they sprout. Continue mulching beds to keep soil cool and weeds down.

GROUNDCOVER

There is still time to cut back Asian jasmine with a weed trimmer. This is a good time to thin the monkey grass and liriope borders. Use the excess to make new borders or share with a friend. Purchasing ground cover can be a major expense in planting beds.

LAWN

Apply broadleaf weed control in lawns that need it. Fertilize all lawns with a slow release turf fertilizer in mid-April.

ROSES

Roses are coming into full bloom and will be at their peak in the middle of the month. It is best to cut in the early morning or late afternoon.

Do not cut an open flower as it will soon shatter. Instead, choose a tight bud at the stage when the small, green sepals at the bottom have begun to peel back. Carry a bucket of water and immerse stems immediately. Use sharp shears or knife and cut at a 45 degree angle, 1/4 inch above a 5-leaflet joint. When putting them into a vase, re-cut and remove lower leaves. A flower preservative will make them last longer. Add fresh water daily as it evaporates. Change water every other day.

TREES AND SHRUBS

Spray trunks of trees susceptible to borers (flowering cherry, cherry-laurel, ash and river birch).

Thin fruit on peach and nectarine trees in mid-April to a spacing of one every 8 inches.

Blueberries will be in bloom and should be re-fertilized each year with an acid-forming fertilizer.

This is the month to prune azalea plants. Take out dead wood and branches that are overgrown or seem out of place. Maintain the natural form of the plant by staggering the height of the pruning cuts. Fertilize and check for lacebug damage. Prune other spring flowering shrubs, such as spirea, by cutting out 1/3 of the older and less vigorous canes.

Spray for forest tent caterpillar and buck moth (stinging caterpillar) larvae while they are still young. Repeat spraying one week later.

VEGETABLES

Harvest strawberries. Tomato plants will begin to blossom in April, promising a succulent crop soon. Four weeks after transplanting vegetables, side dress with ammonium nitrate fertilizer. This will stimulate them into vigorous growth. Apply mineral oil or Sevin to corn silks to help control corn earworm.

FIRST WEEK

Continue planting spring vegetables.

Plant caladium bulbs through May.

Thin peach fruit to one every 8 inches.

Spray pecan trees for phylloxera fungus.

SECOND WEEK

Roses should be at their peak.

Fertilize turf grass with a slow-release nitrogen application.

THIRD WEEK

Selectively prune azalea plants.

Thin fruits on your fruit trees.

Side-dress vegetables with ammonium nitrate.

FOURTH WEEK

Spray trees to prevent stem-borer damage.

Lagniappe
Plant mint in large flower pots or whiskey barrels to keep it from invading the rest of your garden.

See charts in back of book

Bloom
*indicates best bloomers

ANNUALS

Ageratum
Amaranthus
Begonia
Celosia
Coleus
Columbine
Cosmos, yellow
Dianthus*
Foxglove*
Geranium*
Hollyhock*
Impatiens
Larkspur
Lisianthus
Marigold
Nicotiana
Pentas
Periwinkle*
Phlox drummondii, annual
Garden Poppy*
Salvia
Snapdragon*
Strawflower
Sweet Pea*
Zinnia

BULBS

Agapanthus
Alstroemeria
Amaryllis*
Calla Lily
Hymenocallis
Dutch Iris
Louisiana Iris*
Tiger Lily

PERENNIALS, *shade or sun*

Echinacea
Hosta
Louisiana Phlox
Blue Salvia
Spiderwort
Stokesia

PERENNIALS *sun only*

Coreopsis
Lantana
Rudbeckia
Shasta Daisy
Verbena*
Veronica

VINES

Allamanda
Confederate Jasmine

TREES AND SHRUBS

Azalea
Citrus
Crabapple
Dogwood
Indian Hawthorne
Magnolia
Roses
Spirea

Seed

FLOWERS

Abelmoschus
Amaranthus
Balsam
Celosia
Cleome
Cosmos
Four O'clock
Globe Amaranth
Native Hibiscus
Periwinkle
Zinnia

The flowering dogwood is native to much of the eastern United States.

VEGETABLES AND HERBS

Butter Bean
Pole Bean
Cantaloupe
Cucumber
Okra
Southern Peas
Pepper
Pumpkin
Watermelon

Transplant

Abelmoschus
Ageratum
Allamanda
Amaranth
Begonia
Blue Daze
Caladium
Celosia
Cleome
Coleus
Cosmos, yellow
Dwarf Dahlia
Echinacea
Gaillardia
Geranium
Gladiolus
Globe Amaranth
Tropical Hibiscus
Native Hibiscus
Impatiens
Jacobinia
Lisianthus
Mandevilla
Marigold

Mexican Heather
Nicotiana
Pentas
Ornamental Pepper
Periwinkle
Purslane
Rudbeckia
Salvia
Thunbergia
Torenia
Zinnia

VEGETABLES AND HERBS

Cantaloupe
Cucumber
Eggplant
Mirliton
Okra
Pepper
Squash
Tomato
Watermelon

Harvest

Broccoli
Carrot
Lettuce
Parsley
English Peas
Potato
Shallot
Spinach
Strawberry

HISTORIC NOTE

Gumbo

Gumbo, one of the most original creations of Louisiana cuisine, developed from specialties of the Africans, Indians and Creoles. It was served on every occasion at the tables of rich and poor alike - even in soup houses in town. The soup, gumbo, could be made with any game or domestic fowl, meat, seafood or a combination thereof. A family reunion in 1803 included 24 kinds of gumbo in its menu.

Gumbo also referred to the vegetable okra/ocra/ochre itself. It could be served boiled, buttered and seasoned with salt and pepper. When cooked it has a thready quality. This particular quality of gumbo – vegetable or soup, came to be its chief characteristic. The Creoles adopted, from the Choctaw Indians, the use of dried, finely ground sassafras leaves which they called filé, meaning "thready." Consequently any number of soups, with okra or with filé, came to be known as gumbo.

From *The Magnolia Mound Plantation Kitchen Book, Being a Compendium of Foodways and Customs of Early Louisiana 1795-1841*, Composed by Dedicated Friends of Magnolia Mound Plantation, Magnolia Mound Plantation House, 1986, p. 14.

*M*ay has three passwords and they are water, water, water. It's an excellent time to plan for the hot summer ahead by installing a low-pressure or trickle irrigation system to an outside faucet. This is the transition time between spring and summer bloomers and separates the dabblers from the true gardeners. Many annuals that look great in spring, such as petunias and geraniums, do not thrive in a tropical summer climate.

The delicious scents of magnolia and gardenia blossoms fill the air and hydrangeas will visually "cool" a shady retreat. Consider doing some planting in hanging baskets or buy them already done. They can be moved around and grouped for color, size and texture combinations. Just remember to fertilize them frequently, preferably every other week, with a soluble fertilizer. Some salvia that may work well in your garden are salvia superba (blue, pink, rose), salvia greggii (hot pink, white, coral) and salvia azurea grandflora (blue).

Add ferns to the garden in shadier spots. They provide a good contrast for your flowers and an "appearance" of coolness. It just doesn't seem as hot when looking out on a fern bed. Some types to try are holly, autumn, cinnamon and maidenhair. Use extra lime with the maidenhair.

CULTURE

Kill summer weeds before they seed. Continue your battle against spider mites, aphids and caterpillars and protect small flowering plants with a slug bait. Mulching beds will lessen your need for watering, moderate the soil temperature and help control weeds.

How Much Mulch?

3 cu. ft. bag mulch covers 12 sq. ft. when spread 3" deep

3 cu. ft. bag mulch covers 18 sq. ft. when spread 2" deep

3 cu. ft. bag mulch covers 36 sq. ft. when spread 1" deep

1 cu. yd. = 27 cu. ft.

1 cu. yd. covers 108 sq. ft. when spread 3" deep

1 cu. yd. covers 162 sq. ft. when spread 2" deep

1 cu. yd. covers 324 sq. ft. when spread 1" deep

When summer annuals have been in the ground about two months, give them a second application of fertilizer. The liquid hose-end type is convenient and results are almost immediate, but the other types (granular, slow-release) are also good. Many spring annuals, including pansy and sweet pea, should be removed to make way for the heat lovers.

Phalaenopsis orchids would benefit by "summering" them outside in shade. Be sure to raise the pot off the ground or snails and outside roaches will make fast food of the tender young leaves.

Ligustrum fills the air with its fragrance. If this is overwhelming and bushes are not too big, shear them back before the flowers open.

PERENNIALS

Stake tall perennials before they need support. Allow them to grow over or through the support. Many times stokesias will re-bloom if you remove the flower stalks. Start spraying for leaf rollers on canna lilies.

ROSES

Roses are in fragrant, glorious bloom now. Try adding a few annuals, like purslane, to rose and perennial beds for extra color. Visit local public gardens. Make notes of varieties to add to the garden.

LAWN

Can't decide on whether to choose St. Augustine or centipede? Consider the advantages of each.

St. Augustine has a rich blue-green color that is tolerant of both shade and heat. It maintains some green coloring during most winters. Centipede has a yellow-green color that usually turns completely brown during the winter. It has a fair tolerance for shade but also tolerates the heat well.

St. Augustine grass is established by sodding or plugging. Summer mowing height should be 1 1/2 to 2 1/2 inches. Centipede may be established through sodding, plugging or seeding, but it has a slower rate of growth. Establishing a centipede lawn by plugging or seeding may take some time but averages about one dollar cheaper per square yard. Mow 1 to 2 inches high.

Diseases and insects that affect St. Augustine are brown patch, dollar spot, St. Augustine decline and chinch bugs. Brown patch is the only disease that affects centipede.

TREES AND SHRUBS

The magnolia will start shedding its old leaves so don't be alarmed. This is an annual occurrence. Wait a while to prune live oaks. Studies have shown that a wilt may be transmitted if trees are pruned now. Harvest the Southern cherry in mid-May for bounce or jellies. Fertilize azaleas with azalea-camellia food.

VINES

Take this month to enhance the garden with a few vines along fences, railings and walls. Choose from allamanda, blackeyed Susan, bleeding heart, bougainvillea, clematis, cypress vine, Mexican flame vine, gloriosa lily, Confederate jasmine, Carolina jasmine or jessamine, mandevilla, moonvine, morning glory and rose-of-Montana.

VEGETABLES

To prolong harvest, pick vegetables frequently. If any are allowed to over ripen, the plant will cease to produce. Spray for squash vine borer.

FIRST WEEK

Install a trickle irrigation system in the landscape.

SECOND WEEK

Apply a post-emergent lawn herbicide. Be sure it is labeled specifically for the chosen grass and do not apply over the root zones of trees and shrubs.

THIRD WEEK

Control powdery mildew on crape myrtles.

Harvest Southern cherries for cherry bounce.

FOURTH WEEK

Plan a garden to attract butterflies and hummingbirds.

Lagniappe

May is an excellent month to visit local gardens featuring perennial, rose, annual and herb gardens in full swing.

See charts in back of book

Bloom
*indicates best bloomers

ANNUALS

Ageratum
Balsam
Begonia*
Celosia
Coleus
Cosmos, yellow
Dianthus
Foxglove
Geranium*
Globe Amaranth
Hollyhock*
Impatiens*
Larkspur
Lisianthus
Marigold*
Nicotiana
Pansy
Pentas
Petunia*
Purslane
Salvia*
Snapdragon
Sweet Pea
Sweet William
Verbena
Zinnia*

BULBS

Agapanthus
Alstroemeria
Amaryllis
Caladium
Calla Lily
Canna
Crinum
Dahlia
Gladiolus
Hymenocallis
Louisiana Iris
Tiger Lily

PERENNIALS

"Cashmere Bouquet"
Coreopsis
Daylily*
Echinacea
Four O'clock
Gaillardia
Gerbera Daisy
Native Hibiscus
Hosta
Jacobinia
Confederate Jasmine
Lantana
Loosestrife
Summer Phlox
Plumbago
Rudbeckia*
Blue Salvia*
Shasta Daisy*
Stokesia

Verbena
Veronica
Yarrow

TREES AND SHRUBS

Azalea, late
Gardenia*
Hydrangea*
Magnolia*
Oleander
Plumbago
Rose*

Seed

Amaranthus
Balsam
Celosia
Cleome
Cosmos, yellow
Four O'clock
Zinnia

VEGETABLES AND HERBS

Butter Bean
Pole Snap Bean
Cantaloupe
Okra
Southern Peas
Pumpkin
Watermelon

Transplant

Abelmoschus
Allamanda
Amaranth
Blue Daze
Celosia
Cleome
Coleus
Croton
Copperplant
Echinacea
Gaillardia
Globe Amaranth
Tropical Hibiscus
Native Hibiscus
Impatiens
Mandevilla
Marigold
Pentas
Ornamental Pepper
Periwinkle
Purslane
Rose-of-Montana
Rudbeckia
Thunbergia
Torenia
Zinnia

VEGETABLES AND HERBS

Eggplant
Okra
Pepper

Harvest

Beans
Carrot
Corn
Cucumber
Dill
Garlic
Onion
Potato
Shallot
Squash

Though a challenge to cultivate in the South, artichokes are grown at Magnolia Mound Plantation's historic kitchen garden for their edible buds and their spectacular flowers. French immigrants brought artichokes to the American South in the early 19th century, but the plants do best in a cooler climate.

June reveals summer blossoms at their peak of color and variety. Real scene-stealers are the crape myrtles and mimosas. Caladiums, impatiens and daylilies are in their prime. Preserve this beauty as long as possible by continuing insect and weed control, as well as watering regularly if rains are infrequent. Remember that pots, especially small pots, may need watering every day or more. Get references and several itemized bids or consultations before deciding on landscape or tree work.

PLANT

It is still not too late to plant plumbago. It needs full sun to bloom well. Try it in a raised planter with asparagus fern where both can weep over the edge. Petunias usually play out once the nights get hot. If they look bad, throw them away and replace with a hot season flower. Leather leaf fern is a beautiful plant for those shady areas and the leaves can be used for floral arrangements. Severe winters will kill them but it is worth the risk.

CULTURE

Weeds can take over beds very quickly when summer rains are plentiful. It is very important to keep beds free of weeds. They compete for sunlight and nutrition as well as harbor insects and diseases. To prevent this, keep a thick mulch on beds. Spray where you are able with an herbicide. Be careful. Chemicals can do more damage to plants than weeds could ever do. When using a new chemical, spray a small area to test and wait 10 days to assess results.

Continue deadheading. In plants with many tiny blossoms it is easier to shear off the top few inches of the plant. This technique works well on coleus, coreopsis, torenia, echinacea and verbena.

Zinnias are susceptible to both powdery mildew and blight. Powdery mildew is the white powdery film that develops on the tops of leaves. Blight (reddish spots) spreads quickly and causes holes in the leaves. Spray leaves with appropriate fungicides weekly or bi-weekly. Root pruning may enhance the blooming of an unproductive older wisteria.

PERENNIALS

Although the perennial garden is starting to fill in, new plants may still be added where needed. Garden centers have a good selection of containerized plants to choose from.

ROSES

Sawflies leave half-moon holes on leaves. The best means of control is sanitation. Keep off dead leaves and prune dead stems. Continue a spray program.

GROUNDCOVER

Keep Asian jasmine out of shrubs. It will twine in them and become a mess. Re-fertilize all ground covers except English ivy. Be on the lookout for fungal leaf spot.

LAWN

Watch for chinch bugs in St. Augustine and treat immediately. Damage looks like irregular patches of brown grass. It is usually found in dry, sunny areas and often originates near curbs, sidewalks or buildings. Chinch bugs are active from June through September. If there are brown patches during summer, it's probably from chinch bugs. To control chinch bugs without using insecticides, water and fertilize properly and manage thatch. Add chemical insecticides only when necessary.

TREES AND SHRUBS

Control aphids on crape myrtles. Plant palms through August. Thin fruit on fruit trees to produce larger fruit. Eliminate root suckers. Remove fallen, decaying fruit to prevent harboring pests.

The summer harvest continues with fruit on blackberry, blueberry, crabapple, fig, peach, nectarine and plum trees.

Buds on spring-flowering shrubs are formed in May and June so keep plants well watered and don't prune after June. Prune while blooming and use the flowers in arrangements or prune immediately after the flowers fade.

DRYING AND PRESERVING

Cut hydrangea blossoms as the heads begin to age but while the color is still strong. Hang upside down for a few weeks. White and yellow yarrows can be dried in the same way.

FIRST WEEK

Can fresh vegetables and fruits for later use.

Cut young magnolia blossoms. They last longer and bruise less easily.

Add mulch to beds to control weeds and conserve moisture.

SECOND WEEK

Prune freeze-damaged limbs on citrus and other trees and shrubs.

Remove watersprouts and other unwanted branches on fruit trees.

THIRD WEEK

Throw away petunias and other spring annuals and replace with heat tolerant plants like periwinkle and purslane.

Prune old fruiting canes of blackberries after harvest.

FOURTH WEEK

It is not too late to plant or replant zinnias and cosmos.

Cut back basil by half. Put in food processor with a little olive oil and save in the refrigerator.

Lagniappe

Giving a dried wedding bouquet to a newly married couple is a wonderful way to preserve special memories. To dry the bouquet dismantle the arrangement and put in a plastic bag and place in the refrigerator for about an hour. Remove from the refrigerator and immediately press between newspapers to retain the colors. Place under something that is very heavy for several weeks. Garden flowers that were blooming at the time of the wedding or fern sprigs may be added. Purchase an oval frame and use fabric from the bridal gown or border in antique lace for the backing. Be creative in arranging the flowers. Don't try to recreate the original bouquet. Add small mementos that the bride can treasure.

See charts in back of book

Bloom
indicates best bloomers

ANNUALS

Abelmoschus
Ageratum
Amaranthus
Balsam
Begonia*
Blue Daze
Celosia*
Cleome
Coleus
Cosmos
Croton
Dianthus
Geranium
Globe Amaranth
Mexican Heather
Tropical Hibiscus
Impatiens*
Ixora
Larkspur
Lisianthus
Marigold*
Melapodium
Nicotiana
Pentas
Ornamental Pepper
Periwinkle*
Purslane*
Salvia
Statice
Sunflower
Torenia
Zinnia*

BULBS

Agapanthus
Caladium*
Calla Lily
Canna
Crinum
Dahlia
Gladiolus
Hymenocallis
Formosa Lily
Tiger Lily
Montbretia

PERENNIALS

Angel Trumpet
Hardy Begonia
Butterfly Weed
"Cashmere Bouquet"
Coreopsis
Daylily*
Echinacea
Four O'clock
Gaillardia
Gerbera Daisy
Native Hibiscus
Hosta
Jacobinia
Lantana*
Liriope
Loosestrife*
Summer Phlox
Plumbago
Rudbeckia
Blue Salvia*
Salvia Guarinatica
Shasta Daisy
Stokesia
Pennisetum
Verbena
Veronica
Yarrow

VINES

Allamanda
Honeysuckle
Mandevilla
Passionflower

TREES AND SHRUBS

Althea
Butterfly Bush
Crape Myrtle*
Hydrangea
Oakleaf Hydrangea
Oleander*
Magnolia
Mimosa
Vitex
Yesterday, Today and Tomorrow

Seed

Amaranthus
Balsam
Celosia
Cleome
Cosmos
Four O'clock
Globe Amaranth
Native Hibiscus
Periwinkle
Zinnia

VEGETABLES

Butter Bean
Collards
Pumpkin
Tomato

Transplant

Abelmoschus
Allamanda
Amaranthus
Blue Daze
Celosia
Caladium
Cleome
Coleus
Copperplant
Coreopsis
Cosmos
Croton
Echinacea
Gaillardia
Globe Amaranth
Tropical Hibiscus
Impatiens
Jacobinia
Mandevilla
Marigold
Melapodium
Mexican Heather
Nicotiana
Periwinkle
Purslane
Rose-of-Montana
Rudbeckia
Thunbergia
Torenia
Zinnia

Harvest

Butterbean
Snap Bean
Lima Bean
Cantaloupe
Corn
Cucumber
Eggplant
Okra
Southern Peas
Peppers
Squash
Tomato
Watermelon

Fresh basil and sliced tomatoes from the garden with a sprinkling of olive oil, balsamic vinegar, salt and ground pepper make a delightfully refreshing summer salad.

HISTORIC NOTE

Receipt for Summer Beer

Take four quarts of molasses, half a pint of yeast, and a spoonful of powdered race ginger; put the ingredients into your vessel, and pour on them two gallons of scalding hot water; shake them well till it ferments, and add thirteen gallons of cold water, to fill up the cask. Let the liquor ferment about twelve hours, when it will be fit for use. It may be kept in the bottles to a great age.

Baton Rouge Gazette

From *The Magnolia Mound Plantation Kitchen Book, Being a Compendium of Foodways and Customs of Early Louisiana 1795-1841*, Composed by Dedicated Friends of Magnolia Mound Plantation, Magnolia Mound Plantation House, 1986, p. 58.

July is the time when the deep summer heat sets in. Remember that plants demand plenty of water. During dry spells, supplement with one to three good soakings per week. Most annuals are still in bloom if they have been sufficiently watered and fertilized.

Make a point to notice where sunny and shady spots are in the yard to plant shade trees or put in a new sunny garden area. Plan a fall/winter garden now and order seed for sowing in August and September.

CULTURE

Gingers are carefree plants with exotic blooms which make beautiful cut flowers. Some recommended varieties are white butterfly, salmon, purple pineapple and yellow.

This is the month to plant chrysanthemums for the best fall showing. Plant two varieties for an extended bloom.

Divide bearded iris now. Cut back echinacea, rudbeckia, dahlias and annuals to induce good fall blossoms.

Some annuals, such as marigolds, zinnias and celosias, may need to be replaced with young transplants for blooms through the fall. Check globe amaranth for caterpillar infestations.

This is a good month to divide spider lily bulbs. Re-fertilize caladiums to keep them growing vigorously.

Harvest the seed from daylily, echinacea, iris and stokesia.

PERENNIALS AND HERBS

Notice any clashing colors or boring compositions for later change. Deadhead perennials and keep beds weed free.

ROSES

It is time to order from mail order catalogs or local nurserymen for January/February delivery. Buy #1 grade rose bushes.

GROUNDCOVER

Use the blooms from liriope for an interesting color and texture in summer flower arrangements.

LAWN

Apply a second application of slow release fertilizer as recommended for the chosen variety of grass. Continue mowing centipede at about 1 1/2 inches and St. Augustine at about 2 1/2 inches.

TREES AND SHRUBS

Hydrangea and abelia are in bloom, as well as crape myrtle, vitex and magnolia. Cut back old blossoms on crape myrtle to prolong blooms. Watch for sooty mold and aphids on all trees. Prune hydrangeas now and adjust color. Ammonium sulfate will turn them bluer and lime will turn them pinker.

VEGETABLES

Keep well weeded and adequately watered. When spring vegetables die back, plow under plant debris or remove from the garden to minimize disease buildups. Till and fertilize. When planting a fall garden, don't plant the same vegetables in the same rows in which they were planted last spring. Compost debris.

MICROWAVE DRYING

Cut the flower stem 1 1/4 inches below the blossom. A wooden toothpick should be stuck through the bottom of the flower for those with thin, fragile stems. Layer 1 1/4 inches of silica gel on the bottom of a wooden or cardboard box (not metal!) Place flowers in an upright position and fill 1 1/4 inches of silica gel between the container sides and the flowers. Place container uncovered on an elevated microwave drain rack and set on medium low.

Drying time varies:

2 minutes for 1/2 pound

5 minutes for 2 pounds

7 minutes for 3 pounds

Home experimentation will be necessary for various flowers. Practice first on single petaled flowers like daisies. Rosebuds require more skill. After microwaving, the material must stand from 10 minutes for fragile flowers to 30 minutes for sturdy flowers. Gently remove flowers from the container and either shake off the excess silica gel or brush with a small paintbrush.

To reuse the silica gel, sift out left-over flower parts, place in microwave and set on medium high. Stir every few minutes until granules turn from pink to blue (about 10 minutes). Re-dry gel 2 pounds at a time. Although silica gel is non-toxic, always clean the microwave after use. Bring a cup of water with a dash of lemon juice to boil in the microwave. Set on low and boil for 3 minutes. Thoroughly dry the inside and the door.

FIRST WEEK

Treat the home and lawn for fleas before leaving for vacation.

Dry hydrangea blossoms.

SECOND WEEK

Check St. Augustine grass for chinch bugs.

Re-treat crape myrtles for insects that cause sooty mold.

Transplant mums.

THIRD WEEK

Cut back daylilies severely (about 4") to remove spent flower stalks and old foliage.

FOURTH WEEK

Cut back leggy annuals.

Prune hydrangeas and add soil amendments now for a new color next year.

Flowers such as roses, marigolds, zinnias, goldenrod, yarrow and hydrangeas are readily available and dry well in the microwave.

**See charts in
back of book**

Bloom
***indicates best
bloomers***

ANNUALS

Abelmoschus
Amaranthus
Balsam
Begonia
Blue Daze
Butterfly Bush
Celosia
Cleome
Coleus
Copperplant
Coreopsis
Cosmos, purple
Cosmos, yellow
Croton
Gaillardia
Gerbera
Globe Amaranth*
Tropical Hibiscus
Impatiens*
Ixora
Lisianthus
Marigold
Mandevilla
Melapodium
Mexican Heather
Nicotiana
Pentas
Ornamental Pepper
Periwinkle
Purslane
Salvia
Sunflower
Tithonia
Torenia
Zinnia

BULBS

Achimenes
Agapanthus
Caladium*
Canna
Crinum*
Ginger*
Gladiolus
Hymenocallis
Montbretia
Formosa Lily
Rain Lily
Tiger Lily

SHADE-BLOOMING PERENNIALS

"Cashmere Bouquet"
Hardy Begonia
Four O'clock
Jacobinia
Jewels of Opar
Blue Salvia
Stokesia

PERENNIALS

Angel Trumpet
Butterfly Weed
Coreopsis
Daylily
Echinacea
Gaillardia
Gerbera Daisy
Native Hibiscus*
Jacobinia*
Jewels of Opar
Lantana*
Liriope

Lisianthus
Loosestrife*
Pennisetum
Summer Phlox*
Physostegia
Plumbago
Rudbeckia
Salvia guarinatica
Verbena
Veronica
Yarrow

VINES

Allamanda
Honeysuckle
Mandevilla
Morning Glory*
Moonvine
Passionvine
Gloriosa Lily
Rose-of-Montana

TREES AND SHRUBS

Althea*
Butterfly Bush
Crape Myrtle*

Seed

FLOWERS

Amaranthus
Balsam
Cosmos, purple
Cosmos, yellow
Marigold
Zinnia

VEGETABLES AND HERBS

Cabbage
Cantaloupe, late
Cauliflower, late
Leeks
Melons
Tomato

Transplant

VEGETABLES AND HERBS

Tomato

Harvest

VEGETABLES AND HERBS

Butter Bean
Lima Bean
Pole Bean
Cantaloupe
Corn
Cucumber
Eggplant
Okra
Southern Peas
Pepper
Tomato
Squash
Watermelon

One of the first cultivated crops in the Americas, peppers have been a part of the diet for more that 9000 years. Columbus was one of the first Europeans to experience peppers in the Caribbean. Hot peppers and their cultivars are now grown around the world and are used for medicinal purposes as well as in cooking.

A Monthly Gardening Guide for the Gulf South   35

HISTORIC NOTE

Lapereaux aux Fines Herbes

Cut and prepare your young rabbit - put in with fine herbs chopped very fine and cook in a casserole with a little butter, parsley and green onions tied together, shallots and mushrooms chopped. When the rabbit is done, remove the tied bouquet. Skim off the fat from the sauce and add the juice of a lemon or a small amount of verjus.

Tante Huppe

From *The Magnolia Mound Plantation Kitchen Book, Being a Compendium of Foodways and Customs of Early Louisiana 1795-1841*, Composed by Dedicated Friends of Magnolia Mound Plantation, Magnolia Mound Plantation House, 1986, p.37.

August is an excellent time to prepare beds for fall planting. Cutting back annuals and re-fertilizing may extend and renew the blooms on some plants. Pull out plants that look tired and spent. August is hot so don't forget to thoroughly water the garden and lawn if rains are scarce.

Late season bloomers are beginning to come into their glory now. What could be prettier that pineapple sage's bright red flowers covered with yellow sulfur butterflies and hummingbirds!

CULTURE

Continue replenishing the mulch in your flower beds. This will help keep the weeds down and the soil cool and retain soil moisture.

Remember to keep caladiums well watered.

Divide overcrowded clumps of daylilies and Louisiana iris. Cut back to a few inches if unsightly.

ROSES

Mid-August is the time to prune roses. This will prepare them for their fall bloom. First cut back any stems with die-back. Cut out any crossing branches. Prune to a height of 3 feet for hybrid teas and just lightly for grandifloras and floribundas.

Care must be taken not to remove too many of the leaves as these are needed for photosynthesis. Shape the miniatures lightly. Make cuts 3/4 inch above a bud, pruning so that the top bud faces outward from the plant. If canker die-back is suspected, dip pruners in alcohol or 10% Clorox solution. Fertilize after pruning to encourage new growth. See page 74 for recommendations.

Kitchen docents, Rosemary Lane and Beverly Hadnot, demonstrate cooking in the 1800s.

LAWN

Apply granulated fungicide to control brown patch. Brown patch damage looks like large circular patches of yellow or brown grass. The outer edges are yellowish-brown, but the inside of the circle often remains green. A patch growing through cool weather is probably this fungus. If this problem has been present during last fall or winter, the lawn should be treated the last part of this month even if it appears to have disappeared during warmer weather.

VEGETABLES

Leave peppers, eggplants and okra in your garden. They will continue producing through the fall.

PRESERVING WITH GLYCERIN

Use glycerin preservation for magnolias, camellias, hollies, iris, ivies, maple, oak and eucalyptus. In August and early fall, pick mature leaves and branches up to 2 feet long. Remove the bark from the bottom 2 inches of thick branches and cut angled slices deep into the stem to enlarge the absorption surface. Place the cut ends in 1 1/2 inch deep solution of 1 part glycerin to 2 parts warm water. Store in a warm room to soak for a least 2 to 3 weeks. Remove from solution, hang on clothesline to drip, rinse with warm water and pat with paper towels.

DRYING

Gather and dry garden and roadside flowers for fall and winter arrangements. See July for microwave drying.

FIRST WEEK

Harvest everlastings (see page 62) such as celosia and globe amaranth.

SECOND WEEK

Watch for spider lilies. The blossoms will be emerging now so be careful not to cut them off.

THIRD WEEK

Prune hybrid tea roses.

Start harvesting muscadine grapes now through October.

FOURTH WEEK

Apply brown patch control.

Lagniappe

POTPOURRI RECIPE

1-1/2 teaspoons ground cinnamon

1-1/2 teaspoons ground orris root

3 to 4 cloves

1 drop patchouli oil, optional

6 drops rose oil

2 drops lavender oil

4 cups dried flowers

Experiment with this formula. Throw in dried slivers of orange or lemon peel. Include a few fragrant leaves like camphor or fresh bay. Try a few fragrant seeds too.

Rose petals are a must. Be sure to dry first before adding to your potpourri or it will mildew. Pastels look better dried. Add pressed brightly colored flowers even if they are scentless. Pansies are a favorite.

The orris root serves as a fixative. Otherwise the scent deteriorates within a few months. It can be found in most craft shops.

**See charts in
back of book**

Bloom
*****indicates best
bloomers**

ANNUALS

Abelmoschus
Amaranthus
Balsam
Begonia
Blue Daze
Celosia
Clemone*
Coleus
Copperplant
Cosmos, purple
Cosmos, yellow
Croton
Gerbera
Globe Amaranth*
Tropical Hibiscus*
Impatiens
Ixora
Marigold
Melapodium
Mexican Heather
Pennisetum
Pentas*
Ornamental Pepper
Periwinkle*
Purslane*
Salvia
Sunflower
Torenia
Zinnia

BULBS

Achimenes
Caladium*
Canna
Ginger*
Rain Lily
Spider Lily*
Montbretia*

PERENNIALS

Angel Trumpet
Hardy Begonia
Butterfly Weed
"Cashmere Bouquet"
Echinacea
Four O'clock*
Gaillardia
Gerbera Daisy
Jacobinia*
Jewels of Opar
Native Hibiscus*
Liriope
Summer Phlox*
Physostegia
Plumbago*
Pineapple Sage*
Rudbeckia*
Salvia guarinatica
Talinum

VINES

Allamanda
Autumn Clematis*
Honeysuckle
Mandevilla*
Moonvine*
Morning Glory*

TREES AND
SHRUBS

Althea
Crape Myrtle

Seed
start seed in peat pot

Alyssum
Flowering Cabbage
and Kale
Calendula
Cosmos, purple
Cosmos, yellow
Dianthus
Hollyhock
Johnny-Jump-Up
Lobelia
Nicotiana
Pansy
Petunia
Phlox drummondi,
annual
Verbena, annual
Zinnia

VEGETABLES
AND HERBS

Snap Bean
Broccoli
Cabbage
Chinese Cabbage
Cauliflower
Lettuce
Mustard Greens
Parsley
Potato, seed potatoes

Transplant

FLOWERS

Begonia
Chrysanthemum
Marigold
Salvia
Zinnia

VEGETABLES
AND HERBS

Tomato
Cauliflower
Shallot

Harvest

VEGETABLES
AND HERBS

Butter Bean
Okra
Southern Peas
Pepper

Plumbago, a native of South Africa, is a popular ornamental plant in warm temperate climates. It has a wide variety of uses such as foundation plantings, in borders, as color masses in beds, as a filler plant, as a formal or informal hedge or in patio containers. Plumbago is not a demanding plant, easy even for the novice gardener, and its long blooming season keeps color in the garden through the summer and into the fall.

HISTORIC NOTE

Medicinal Herbs

Herbs have also played an important role for medicinal purposes. Some historical uses from the Magnolia Mound gardens were:

borage - antidote for snakebite

comfrey - poultice for healing cuts and bruises

garlic - treatment for fever

lavender - antidote for mad dog bites

lemon balm - made into a tea for female complaints

mint - a remedy for indigestion

pennyroyal - insect repellent and another treatment for fever

sage - ingredient in throat gargle

vetiver - moth repellent

September weather may still be summery, but there is usually a hint of cooler air late in the month and the autumn colors are just around the corner. This is a good month to plan and prepare the garden for the winter.

Take a soil sample for fertility and pH testing. Re-apply fertilizer and continue to inspect for insects.

Use this month to begin building up a compost pile with all those leaves that may be thrown away. To construct, set four fence posts to make a square. A four-foot square bin is good for starters. Attach chicken wire or other similar wire to the post to a height of 24 to 30 inches. Wait for the leaves to start falling then collect and store. Compost piles benefit by the addition of lime, soil and fertilizer. This will promote the decomposition of organic matter and break it down faster.

CULTURE

Wait until the end of the month, or even early October, to put in traditional fall plants such as mum, pansy and snapdragon. Rearrange a part of the garden that is not quite coming together. Cut back tall stalks of herbaceous perennials. Put in new plants where needed.

PERENNIALS AND HERBS

Order your spring-blooming bulbs now for October planting or chilling. This is also a good time to order plants unavailable at local nurseries.

Late September and October are good months to prepare new flower beds and start a perennial or herb garden. Drainage is the most important factor to consider when preparing new beds.

Continue to divide daylilies, Louisiana iris and most other spring-blooming perennials. Transplant calla lily, violets and gerbera daisy.

Consider planting perennial herbs such as artemisia, burnet, chives, comfrey, ginger, hyssop, lemon grass, Spanish lavender, Mexican marigold, sweet marjoram, mint (will be invasive), mugwort, oregano, pennyroyal, rosemary, pineapple sage, sage, savory, santolina, shallots, tarragon, tansy, thyme and lemon verbena (half-hardy). Some fall annual herbs are dill, chervil, cilantro and parsley.

ROSES

This is the last month to fertilize roses. This will ensure a flush of blooms next month and then give them time to prepare for winter dormancy.

GROUNDCOVER

Continue to prune Asian jasmine to 6 inches to keep it from becoming too invasive, especially around shrubs. Keep English ivy trimmed off trees. Once it grows beyond the reach of a ladder, it is out of control. If leaf spot is discovered, repeat spraying with tri-basic copper sulfate.

LAWN

Apply a winterizing fertilizer to the lawn to prepare it for the cold weather.

TREES AND SHRUBS

Except for the few borderline tropical shrubs, such as citrus and bottlebrush, fall/winter planting is preferable to spring/summer.

The fragrance of herbs drying on an overhead rack fills the Magnolia Mound Plantation kitchen.

VEGETABLES

Most people don't think about planting a vegetable garden now, but this is the best time for growing many crops. Broccoli, carrots, lettuce and peas produce bigger yields in a fall garden because they like the cooler nights.

Spray all members of the cabbage family to control cabbage loopers.

FIRST WEEK

Buy pots of mums to put in those parts of the garden that need fall color.

Winterize lawn.

SECOND WEEK

Start a fall vegetable garden.

Apply borer control to fruit trees.

THIRD WEEK

Divide Louisiana iris.

Continue picking muscadine grapes.

FOURTH WEEK

Continue to harvest everlastings.

Lagniappe

Herbs have been important in cooking throughout history. Here are some regional combinations you may want to use:

Cajun - shallots or onions, celery, pepper, garlic

Louisiana "Sweet" herbs - basil, parsley, chives, winter savory, thyme, marjoram, mint

French "Fines Herbes" - parsley, thyme, bay leaf, basil

Tex-Mex - onion, chili pepper, cumin, oregano, garlic, coriander

Chinese - ginger, garlic, cilantro, onion, cloves

Mediterranean - oregano, rosemary, mint, allspice

See charts in back of book

Bloom
*indicates best bloomers

ANNUALS

Abelmoschus
Ageratum
Amaranthus
Balsam
Begonia*
Blue Daze
Caladium
Candelabra Plant
Celosia
Cleome*
Coleus
Copperplant
Cosmos, purple
Cosmos, yellow
Croton
Dianthus
Globe Amaranth*
Tropical Hibiscus
Impatiens*
Ixora
Marigold
Melapodium
Mexican Heather
Pentas
Ornamental Pepper*
Periwinkle*
Petunia
Phlox drummondi, annual
Purslane*
Salvia
Sunflower
Talinum
Torenia
Verbena
Zinnia

BULBS

Achimenes
Caladium
Canna
Dahlia
Ginger*
Rain Lily
Spider Lily
Montbretia*

PERENNIALS

Angel Trumpet*
Hardy Begonia
Butterflyweed
"Cashmere Bouquet"
Echinacea
Four O'clock*
Gaillardia
Gerbera Daisy
Native Hibiscus
Sleeping Hibiscus
Jacobinia*
Jewels of Opar
Lantana
Lobelia cardinalis
Pampas Grass*
Pennisetum
Plumbago*
Rudbeckia
Pineapple Sage
Mexican Sage
Blue Salvia
Salvia guarinatica

VINES

Allamanda*
Bougainvillea
Autumn Clematis
Mandevilla*
Moonvine*
Morning Glory*

TREES AND SHRUBS

Althea
Golden Raintree

Seed

Alyssum
Baby's Breath
Flowering Cabbage and Kale
Calendula
Candytuft
English Daisy
Delphinium
Dianthus
Hollyhock
Johnny-Jump-Up
Pansy
Phlox drummondii, annual
Snapdragon
Statice
Sweet William
Verbena

VEGETABLES

Cabbage
Chinese Cabbage
Carrot
Collard
Lettuce
Mustard Greens
English Peas
Snow Peas
Radish
Shallot
Turnip

Transplant
early September

Begonia
Cosmos
Marigold
Purslane
Zinnia

entire month

Flowering Cabbage and Kale
Calendula
Chrysanthemum
Dianthus
Gerbera Daisy
Hollyhock
Nicotiana
Petunia
Phlox drummondii, annual

VEGETABLES

Broccoli
Cabbage
Cauliflower
Lettuce

Harvest

VEGETABLES

Butter Bean
Eggplant
Okra
Southern Peas
Pepper

The okra plant is thought to have originated in the Ethiopian Highlands of Africa. The plant was described by a Spanish traveler who visited Egypt in 1216. Use and cultivation of okra spread eastward and ultimately made its way to the Americas via the slave trade. The large okra flowers add a touch of beauty to a vegetable garden. They are also edible.

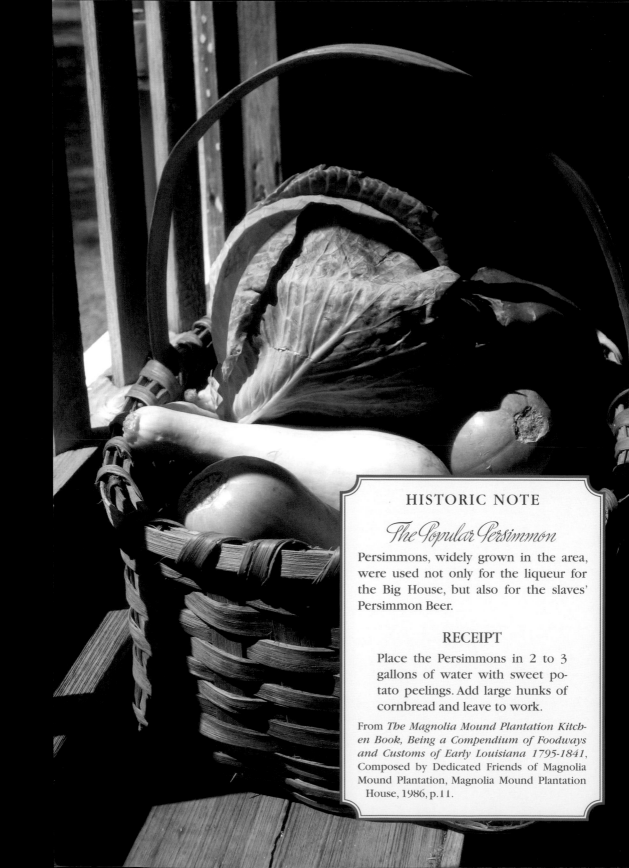

HISTORIC NOTE

The Popular Persimmon

Persimmons, widely grown in the area, were used not only for the liqueur for the Big House, but also for the slaves' Persimmon Beer.

RECEIPT

Place the Persimmons in 2 to 3 gallons of water with sweet potato peelings. Add large hunks of cornbread and leave to work.

From *The Magnolia Mound Plantation Kitchen Book, Being a Compendium of Foodways and Customs of Early Louisiana 1795-1841*, Composed by Dedicated Friends of Magnolia Mound Plantation, Magnolia Mound Plantation House, 1986, p.11.

October is one of the most beautiful, golden months in the south, largely due to the chrysanthemums in brilliant hues. The weather is cooler and warm-season plants are glowing with a last splash of color before giving in to the winter. This is usually the driest month of the year so remember to water the flower beds.

CULTURE

Replant annual beds that are beginning to wane. Some choices for spring blooms are larkspur, poppy, bachelor button, snapdragon and sweet William.

Watch for caterpillars on calendulas and flowering cabbage and kale.

Bougainvillea is in peak bloom now. Protect from freezes and keep in full sun and it will bloom through late spring.

BULBS

This is the month to plan for a bountiful show from spring bulbs next year. Chill tulip and Dutch hyacinth bulbs in the refrigerator vegetable bin at 40 degrees F. for about 8 weeks. Do not put in freezer. They will be ready to plant between mid-December and mid-January. Some recommended varieties:

Red - Apeldoorn, Halcro, King's Blood, President Eisenhower and Oxford

Pink - Pink Supreme, Aristocrat and Elizabeth Arden

Yellow - Golden Apeldoorn and Jewel of Spring

Yellow/Red - Gudoshnik

Spring flowering bulbs such as anemone and ranunculus should be planted this month. Start planting daffodils and narcissus and continue planting them through next month. Some that will repeat are Carlton, Fortune, Thalia, Tete-a-Tete, Paperwhites, Soleil d'Or, Ice Follies, February Gold, Peeping Tom and various jonquils.

October sees the end of caladium growth. Trim back, dig and store the bulbs in dry peat moss, perlite, or coarse vermiculite in a dry frost-free area.

PERENNIALS

Tidy up around plants that are going dormant soon and put in markers to remember their location. Cut back established plants as they begin to die down.

ROSES

Roses are back in full bloom again this month. The colors are even more intense and vibrant due to the cool night temperatures. Don't let up on a spray program as long as leaves remain on the bush.

GROUNDCOVER

Thin liriope and monkey grass borders and use plugs to fill in areas where needed. Groundcovers can greatly improve maintenance, weeding, erosion and water loss. They can also be a lawn substitute or an accent addition.

LAWN

Spread annual ryegrass at a rate 5 to 10 pounds per 1000 square feet. Don't sow thicker than recommended or your regular grass will have difficulty coming through in the spring. Reapply brown patch control.

TREES AND SHRUBS

Fall is the best time for planting trees and shrubs. Select your shrubs for specific purposes:

Framing - Shrubs can provide the framing component to surround a special view. This may require some support from natural or construction features.

Screening - Use evergreens such as ligustrum, photinia, large azaleas or hollies to hide unsightly views.

Accent Plants - Choose a few as focal points but use cautiously.

Plant camellia sasanquas now. Some recommended varieties are Leslie Ann, Yuletide, Pink Snow, Sparkling Burgundy, Bonanza, Shi Shi Gashira, Cotton Candy, Maiden Blush and Snow-on-the-Mountain.

Spray camellias for tea scale. Make sure temperature is not above 80 degrees or below 50 degrees F.

FIRST WEEK
Order strawberries for planting next month.

SECOND WEEK
Harvest herbs to add flavor to cooking. They may also be used for Christmas presents, wreath decorations, potpourri and vinegars.

THIRD WEEK
Chill tulip and hyacinth bulbs.

FOURTH WEEK
Re-treat for brown patch in the lawn.

Butterflies are a beautiful addition to a landscape. To attract adult butterflies looking for nectar, provide blossoms that are red, yellow, orange, pink or purple. They also like flat-topped or clustered flowers. Grow nectar-producing plants, such as zinnias, marigolds and verbenas, in sunny, open areas. Source plants should receive full sun from mid-morning to mid-afternoon as butterflies only feed in the sun.

See charts in back of book

Bloom
*indicates best bloomers

ANNUALS

Abelmoschus
Alyssum
Ageratum
Amaranthus
Balsam
Begonia*
Blue Daze
Calendula
Celosia*
Cleome
Coleus
Copperplant
Cosmos, purple*
Cosmos, yellow*
Croton
Dianthus*
Geranium
Globe Amaranth
Mexican Heather
Tropical Hibiscus
Impatiens*
Johnny-Jump-Up
Marigold
Nicotiana
Pansy
Phlox drummondii,
    annual
Pentas*
Ornamental Pepper*
Periwinkle
Petunia*
Purslane
Salvia*
Snapdragon*
Zinnia

BULBS

Achimenes
Canna
Dahlia
Ginger*

PERENNIALS

Angel Trumpet*
Hardy Begonia
Butterflyweed
Chrysanthemum*
"Cashmere Bouquet"
Echinacea
Four O'clock
Gaillardia
Gerbera Daisy
Native Hibiscus
Jacobinia
Lantana
Plumbago*
Rudbeckia
Mexican Sage*
Blue Salvia
Salvia guarinatica

VINES

Allamanda*
Bougainvillea
Mandevilla
Moonvine*
Morning Glory*

TREES AND SHRUBS

Camellia sasanqua
Roses

Angel trumpets are beautiful, fragrant flowers originating in South America. They usually open after dark and remain open until morning. For the best effect, cultivate the plant into a tree to acquire the most blooms. But beware, this plant is extremely toxic. Do not use in a garden where children play!

Seed

FLOWERS

Alyssum
Baby's Breath
Bachelor Button
Bluebonnet
Columbine
Delphinium
Dianthus
Gerbera Daisy
Johnny-Jump-Up
Larkspur
California Poppy
Garden Poppy
Iceland Poppy
Shirley Poppy
Queen's Anne's Lace
Snapdragon
Statice
Sweet Pea
Sweet William

VEGETABLES

plant seed in ground

Carrot
Garlic
Lettuce, loose leaf
Mustard Greens
Parsley
Radish
Shallot
Spinach
Turnip

Transplant

Alyssum
Ammi majus
Anemone
Flowering Cabbage
    and Kale
Calendula
Daffodil
Dianthus
English Daisy
Foxglove
Hollyhock
Johnny-Jump-Up
Narcissus
Phlox drummondii,
    annual
Ranunculus
Snapdragon
Queen Anne's Lace
Pansy
Petunia
Verbena

Harvest

VEGETABLES

Snap Bean
Butterbean
Cauliflower
Cabbage
Chinese Cabbage
Collards
Eggplant
Mustard Greens
Peppers
Radish
Shallot
Tomato
Turnip

HISTORIC NOTE

To Grill a Fish

After cleaning and scaling your fish, salt, pepper and oil it and let it hang to develop a taste. Put some milt or its roe in butter with some fine herbs. Put this in the opening of your fish and sew it up. Put it on a gridiron over a moderate fire. When done, place it on a plate and serve with a caper sauce or a Maitre d'hôtel sauce.

Tante Huppe

From *The Magnolia Mound Plantation Kitchen Book, Being a Compendium of Foodways and Customs of Early Louisiana 1795-1841*, Composed by Dedicated Friends of Magnolia Mound Plantation, Magnolia Mound Plantation House, 1986, p. 29.

*N*ovember is transition and anticipation. Shift into cool-weather gardening. Prepare ahead for the holidays by sprucing up the yard. The weather is usually pleasantly mild. Consider tackling those projects that weren't completed during the heat. Now you can clean up brush areas or reclaim lost beds.

CULTURE

Many summer annuals will soon die with the first freeze. Remove them and prepare beds for all of the wonderful winter annuals.

Pansies should be given a chance in every garden. They are one of the few flowers that will reliably bloom all through the winter. Choose a sunny location and mass them in beds, pots or hanging baskets. The new colors are vivid and some unusual faces are available.

BULBS

Continue planting spring flowering bulbs during November.

Sometimes caladiums "over winter" and sometimes they don't. If you haven't yet dug up caladium bulbs, remember to do it before the weather gets too cold.

Put paperwhites in shallow pots filled with pea gravel and water. Keep cool and sunny and check water level frequently so that they don't dry out.

PERENNIALS AND HERBS

Ornamental grasses go through several shades of a golden buff. Don't be too hasty in cutting them back now. Enjoy the effect and wait until January or February before removing the old leaves.

Take cuttings of the most tender perennials such as cuphea, datura, jacobinia and salvia. Mulch them to protect from freezing.

ROSES

Early November is a good time to take tip cuttings of roses. This is also the best month to prepare rose beds. Preparing them early allows time for the soil to settle. Be sure to select a site in full sun with good drainage. As an extra precaution, raise the bed 12 to 15 inches. Use 5 parts soil, 4 parts organic matter and 1 part builder's sand. Shredded bark, peat moss, compost, leaf mold and rotted manure are good sources of organic matter. Roses prefer a slight acidic soil with a pH of 6.5. Talk to a county agent about getting your soil tested at a soil testing lab.

GROUNDCOVER

Plant English ivy cuttings now through January to make new beds or increase the size of existing beds. Cut off runners and plant directly in the ground.

LAWNS

To avoid pythium disease, wait until November to overseed the lawn with a perennial ryegrass. Use a blend for best results.

TREES AND SHRUBS

November is a good month to plant all trees except palms (which prefer warm soil) and citrus and figs (which should be planted in early spring). Container-grown trees suffer the least shock when planting as opposed to bare-root or ball-and-burlap prepared trees. Trees will continue to put out roots through the winter and be "set in" when the sap rises for spring growth.

Select trees for hardiness, form, size and availability. Avoid trees that have undesirable characteristics for the chosen location.

See listing on page 75 for recommended fruit tree varieties.

VEGETABLES

During the middle of this month, transplant strawberries.

Broccoli will make several smaller shoots after you cut the central head.

FIRST WEEK

Plant sweet peas.

SECOND WEEK

Put out bait in November to control rodents. They are looking for a good place to spend the winter.

THIRD WEEK

Overseed lawns with perennial ryegrass.

Mulch beds for the holiday season.

FOURTH WEEK

Put paperwhites in pots to have in bloom for Christmas.

Lagniappe

Harvest pecans and other nuts soon after they fall. Nuts left on the ground will absorb moisture causing them to deteriorate.

See charts in back of book

Bloom

indicates best bloomers

+indicates tender annuals

ANNUALS

Alyssum
Begonia+
Flowering Cabbage
  and Kale, late No-
  vember
Calendula*
Celosia+
Cleome+
Coleus+
Copperplant+
Dianthus*
Impatiens+
Johnny-Jump-Up
Marigold+
Mexican Heather+
Nicotiana
Pansy*
Pentas+
Petunia*
Ornamental Pepper+
Phlox drummondii,
  annual*
Snapdragon

PERENNIALS

Butterfly Weed
Chrysanthemum*
Echinacea
Gerbera Daisy
Rudbeckia
Mexican Sage

TREES AND SHRUBS

Abutilon*
Camellia sasanqua*
Japanese Plum
Pyracantha, berries*
Roses
Sweet Olive
Yaupon, berries*

Seed

FLOWERS

plant seed in ground

Bluebonnet
Columbine
Forget-Me-Not
Larkspur
Garden Poppy
Iceland Poppy
Shirley Poppy
Queen Anne's Lace
Sweet Pea

VEGETABLES

plant seed in ground

Carrot
Garlic
Mustard Greens
Radish
Shallots
Spinach
Turnip

Transplant

Alyssum
Anemone
Bachelor Button
Flowering Cabbage
  and Kale
Calendula
Columbine
Daffodil
Dianthus
English Daisy
Forget-Me-Not
Foxglove
Hollyhock
Johnny -Jump-Up
Larkspur
Lobelia
Narcissus
Pansy
Petunia
Garden Poppy
Iceland Poppy
Shirley Poppy
Queen Anne's Lace
Ranunculus
Snapdragon
Statice
Stock
Sweet William
Verbena

Harvest

VEGETABLES AND HERBS

Broccoli
Cabbage
Chinese Cabbage
Cauliflower
Collard
Lettuce
Mustard Greens
English Peas
Snow Peas
Radish
Shallot
Spinach
Turnip

Pyracanthas are grown as ornamental plants for both the flowers and the berries. They may also be used as barriers in a landscape. In a wildlife garden, the pyracantha attracts bees and provides dense vegetation for nesting birds. It has been commonly believed that pyracantha berries are poisonous. However, this is not the case. The berries are edible when cooked and can be used in jellies. Pyracantha jelly is similar to the color and flavor of apple jelly,

HISTORIC NOTE

To Stew Oysters

To stew oysters separate the liquor from them, then wash them from the grit; strain the liquor, and put with them a bit of mace and lemon peel and a few white peppers. Simmer them gently and put some cream and a little flour and butter. Serve with sippets.

Butler Papers

From *The Magnolia Mound Plantation Kitchen Book, Being a Compendium of Foodways and Customs of Early Louisiana 1795-1841*, Composed by Dedicated Friends of Magnolia Mound Plantation, Magnolia Mound Plantation House, 1986, p.28.

December finds the first of the early bulbs, paperwhites and narcissus, in bloom.

Now is the time to collect dried and fresh material for Christmas decorating, such as pine cones, holly branches, rosemary, mistletoe, muscadine vines, sweetgum balls, pyracantha branches, yaupon branches, magnolia leaves, pittosporum, boxwood and Japanese plum.

CULTURE

After the flowers fade on garden chrysanthemums, cut the plants down to about 4 inches.

Mulch tender perennials that were not mulched in November. Some plants that benefit by mulching are hardy begonias, jacobinias and perennial salvias. Mulching may also extend the life of borderline plants such as geranium and Mexican heather.

TREES AND SHRUBS

The beautiful red berries of holly, nandina, ardesia and pyracantha are showing color. Birds have an eye for these tasty winter treats, but except for pyracantha, the berries are toxic to humans and pets.

This is still a good month to plant trees and shrubs. Since nurseries need to make extra room now to carry Christmas trees, many offer plants at attractive discounts.

Recommended Camellia japonica varieties are Gullio Nuccio, Betty Sheffield, Pink Perfection, Pink Debutante, Alba Plena, Dr. Tinsley, Pink Empress, Louisiana Peppermint, R. L. Wheeler, Magnolia flora, Purple Dawn, Rose Dawn, Governor Mouton, Tomor-

In the early 1800s at Magnolia Mound, children set out wooden shoes Christmas Eve in hopes Père Nöel would fill them with rare fresh fruit and other treats.

row, Drama Girl, Vulcan, Bea Rogers, Cold, Granada, Lady Laura Tiffany and Ville de Nantes.

Winter honeysuckle is in bloom now. It is a nice arching shrub that covers itself with white, very fragrant flowers.

POINSETTIAS

For potted plants, keep the soil moist and temperatures moderately warm. Do not let water hit the flowers as it may spot them. Provide bright light but keep out of direct sunlight. Planting outside is not recommended unless special care is taken. Plant on the south side of a sunny wall and expect to protect them from frost a couple of times before Christmas. If a poinsettia bloom breaks off, seal the end with a flame before putting it in water.

CHRISTMAS TREE CARE

1. Make a fresh cut and put in water.
2. Keep outside until ready to decorate.
3. Spray with an anti-desiccant.
4. Always keep the base of the tree in fresh water.
5. Add commercial tree preservatives to prolong freshness or mix your own.

A home recipe is 2 tablespoons Clorox, 1/2 gallon water, 1 1/2 teaspoons liquid iron and 8 tablespoons Karo syrup.

VEGETABLES

Twist cabbage to break some roots. This will delay over maturity and help prevent splitting of the head.

ROSES

Begin to prepare rose beds. See rose hints in November.

FIRST WEEK

Mulch citrus to protect the graft union.

SECOND WEEK

Take potted citrus inside to protect and force into early blooming.

THIRD WEEK

Start to air-layer house plants for separation in spring.

Sliced kumquats with almonds and sugar make a great sauce for duck or pork.

FOURTH WEEK

Plant tulip and hyacinth bulbs through early January.

Merry Christmas!

Lagniappe

Give a potted plant for the holiday season – perhaps an ornamental pepper, forced azalea, kalanchoe or traditional poinsettia. Or buy a tree or shrub for the yard. Books, tools, garden magazine subscriptions and nursery gift certificates found beneath the Christmas tree will also be welcomed.

Poinsettias, native to Central America and Mexico, were called cuetlaxochitl by the Aztecs. They were introduced into the United States in 1825 by Joel Poinsett, the first U.S. Ambassador to Mexico. See page 53 for how to care for poinsettias.

**See charts in
back of book**

Bloom
***indicates best
bloomers**

ANNUALS

Alyssum
Begonia
Flowering Cabbage
    and Kale*
Calendula*
Dianthus*
Johnny-Jump-Up
Pansy*
Phlox drummondii,
    annual
Dwarf Snapdragon

BULBS

Narcissus, Paperwhites
Narcissus, Soleil d'Or

PERENNIALS

Gerbera Daisy

TREES AND
SHRUBS

Abutilon*
Camellia japonica*
Camellia sasanqua*
Winter Honeysuckle
Sweet Olive*

Seed

plant seed in ground
Bachelor Button
Queen Anne's Lace
Sweet Pea, early De-
    cember

start seed in peat pot
Impatiens
Petunia

VEGETABLES
AND HERBS

Carrot
Garlic, transplant
English Peas, late
Radish
Shallot
Spinach
Turnip

Transplant

Early December

Alyssum
Bluebonnet
Columbine
Daffodil
Dianthus
Forget-Me-Not
Foxglove
Hollyhock
Johnny-Jump-Up
Larkspur
Lobelia
Narcissus
Pansy
Garden Poppy
Iceland Poppy
Shirley Poppy
Queen Anne's Lace
Snapdragon
Statice
Sweet William

Late December
Hyacinth
Tulip

Harvest

VEGETABLES
AND HERBS

Broccoli
Cabbage
Chinese Cabbage
Carrot
Cauliflower
Collard
Lettuce
Mustard Greens
English Peas
Snow Peas
Irish Potato
Radish
Shallot
Spinach
Turnip

*Sunlight fills the overseer's
cabin at Magnolia Mound
on a wintry afternoon.*

Landscaping – an Overview

In planning a landscape design, these elements should be considered.

ARCHITECTURAL FORMS

Screen - a plant, plant mass or plants used with other barriers, forming a total enclosure of landscape space that cannot be seen through or walked through

Canopy - a plant or plants with branching height of 7 or more feet, allowing people to walk under

Barrier - a partial enclosure or circulation control, usually 2 to 5 feet high that can be seen over, but not passed through

Baffle - controls the visual experiences within a space, such as a vine on a trellis or groundcover with small trees, that can be seen but not walked through

Groundcover - a plant mass used as a visual floor with a maximum height of 18 inches

LOCATION OF PLANTS

Location consideration

Do not plant trees under utility wires.

Do not plant trees or big shrubs too close to windows, doors, sidewalks or streets.

Do not over plant.

Function

A planting should serve to create an architectural form, such as a screen for privacy, background, scale or visual control or an enclosure for concentration of interest, visual control, privacy or shelter. Lack of an effective enclosure is the key problem in most unsuccessful spaces.

Plant Value

Plants should be located to derive the most value from their color, texture and form. All values are accented by contrast – for instance, a bright color on a pale background, a coarse-textured plant (banana) in a fine-textured bed (ferns), a distinct form (climbing roses) on even surroundings (ligustrum hedge).

Design

Factors to be considered in designing include defining the space, reinforcing the design, complementing the architecture, framing good views, screening undesirable views, controlling movement, providing pleasant sounds, seasonal changes and shadow patterns.

Canopied walkways and trellises add depth and interest to a garden.

Physical Components

Physical factors include temperature, water and light. These factors determine adaptability and hardiness.

FORM

Space

A positive space is enclosed or has a limited field of vision. A negative space is open.

Structure

The shape of a plant or plant mass can be two- or three-dimensional. The shape can be round, oval, conical, upright, horizontal, weeping or irregular. Vertical forms add height and strong accent to a composition. Horizontal forms add width. Weeping forms add soft lines and tie the mass to the ground plane. Conical shapes can be added to rounded forms to prevent monotony. Plants that have similar forms usually go together but only one dominant form should be used.

COLOR

Function of Color

Considered the most striking of design elements in planning a garden, color can attract attention, influence emotions, create a warm or cool atmosphere, add formality or informality, excite and stimulate (bright colors) or evoke restfulness and relaxation (cool colors).

Use of Color

The background (basic color) of the design space should be consistent and pleasing. The accent color should emphasize features that have been chosen for the garden. Use of color is influenced by the viewing distance, light availability and soil conditions.

The versatile impatien makes a bold color statement when planted in masses..

Charts

Although these charts reflect a range for a species, you should not expect the entire length of bloom for a particular plant in your backyard. Let's use azaleas, for example.

To get the entire range of bloom, you should plant early, mid-season, late and fall-blooming varieties. Zinnias will bloom spring through fall, but in order to maintain a tidy appearance, you may need as many as three separate plantings.

The specific time that a plant will begin blooming will vary depending on temperature, water, location and fertilizer.

In addition, many of the Bloom Charts and the Harvest Chart have seeding and transplanting schedules included.

Bloom Chart For Warm & Hot Season Annuals

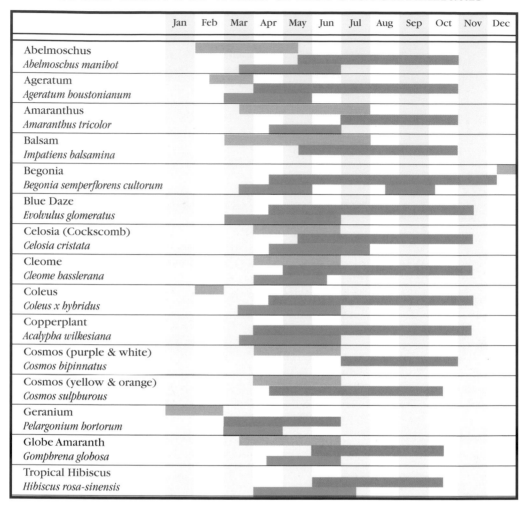

	Jan	Feb	Mar	Apr	May	Jun	Jul	Aug	Sep	Oct	Nov	Dec
Abelmoschus *Abelmoschus manihot*												
Ageratum *Ageratum houstonianum*												
Amaranthus *Amaranthus tricolor*												
Balsam *Impatiens balsamina*												
Begonia *Begonia semperflorens cultorum*												
Blue Daze *Evolvulus glomeratus*												
Celosia (Cockscomb) *Celosia cristata*												
Cleome *Cleome hasslerana*												
Coleus *Coleus x hybridus*												
Copperplant *Acalypha wilkesiana*												
Cosmos (purple & white) *Cosmos bipinnatus*												
Cosmos (yellow & orange) *Cosmos sulphurous*												
Geranium *Pelargonium hortorum*												
Globe Amaranth *Gomphrena globosa*												
Tropical Hibiscus *Hibiscus rosa-sinensis*												

Suggested Flowers and Foliage for Cutting

Agapanthus	Dianthus	Larkspur	Strawflower
Anemone	Dusty Miller, foliage	Liatris	Sweet Pea
Ammi majus	Echinacea	Lisianthus	Tithonia
Bachelor Buttons	Fountain Grass	Loosestrife	Tulip
Bells of Ireland	Gaillardia	Narcissus	Yarrow
Butterfly Bush	Society Garlic	Phlox	
Calendula	Gerbera	Queen Anne's Lace	
Calla Lily	Ginger	Ranunculus	
Celosia	Gladiolus	Rudbeckia	
Chrysanthemum	Globe Amaranth	Salvia farinacea	
Cleome	Gypsophilia	Scabiosa	
Coleus, foliage	Hydrangea	Shasta Daisy	
Cosmos	Iris	Snapdragon	
Dahlia	Jacobinia	Statice	

= Seed

= Bloom

= Transplant

Bloom Chart For Warm & Hot Season Annuals

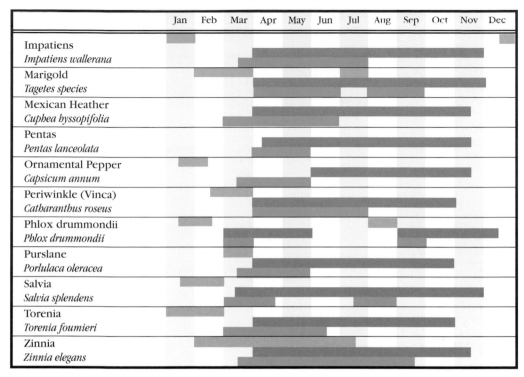

	Jan	Feb	Mar	Apr	May	Jun	Jul	Aug	Sep	Oct	Nov	Dec
Impatiens *Impatiens wallerana*												
Marigold *Tagetes species*												
Mexican Heather *Cuphea hyssopifolia*												
Pentas *Pentas lanceolata*												
Ornamental Pepper *Capsicum annum*												
Periwinkle (Vinca) *Catharanthus roseus*												
Phlox drummondii *Phlox drummondii*												
Purslane *Porlulaca oleracea*												
Salvia *Salvia splendens*												
Torenia *Torenia foumieri*												
Zinnia *Zinnia elegans*												

How to Care for Fresh Cut Flowers

The best time to cut flowers is early in the morning or late afternoon when it is cool.

Flowers cut with a sharp, un-serrated knife and then plunged immediately into luke-warm water keep best. Bulb flowers do best in cold water. Cut on a slant to expose more stem. Remove leaves that would be under water in the vase. Do not remove rose thorns as it may shorten their life.

Maturity also affects the life span of the cut flower. Cut roses, irises, daffodils and gladiolus in the bud stage. Cut marigolds, dianthus and delphiniums when they are open.

A flower's demand for water is continuous. Air bubbles that form at the cut of a stem can block water intake. To clear air bubble blocks, make a new stem cut under water.

Change the water every 2 days. This is the single most effective thing to do to keep flowers fresh.

Keep flowers out of direct sunlight and move to a cool place at night.

Put daffodils in their own vase. They emit a compound that is toxic to other flowers

Keep cut flowers away from fruit which releases a gas that shortens the life of cut flowers.

Use the commercial packets that are available from florists. The packet contains biocides that kill microorganisms. Growth from bacteria, yeast and fungi plug up the tiny tubes in the stems that bring water to the flower. The packets also include an acidifier and sugar.

One of several natural alternatives to using commercial packets is to put a copper penny (acts as a biocide) and an aspirin (makes the water more acidic) into the vase.

Bloom Chart For Cool Season Annuals

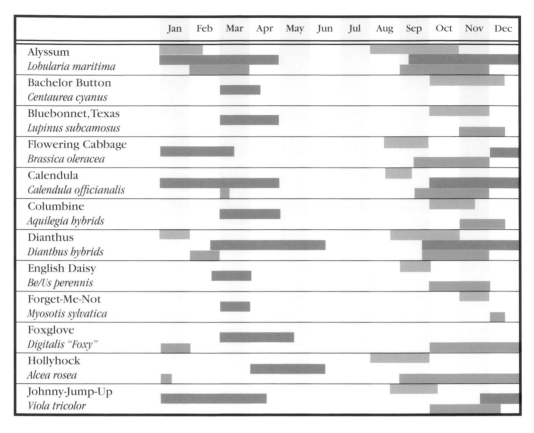

	Jan	Feb	Mar	Apr	May	Jun	Jul	Aug	Sep	Oct	Nov	Dec
Alyssum / *Lobularia maritima*												
Bachelor Button / *Centaurea cyanus*												
Bluebonnet, Texas / *Lupinus subcamosus*												
Flowering Cabbage / *Brassica oleracea*												
Calendula / *Calendula officianalis*												
Columbine / *Aquilegia hybrids*												
Dianthus / *Dianthus hybrids*												
English Daisy / *Be/Us perennis*												
Forget-Me-Not / *Myosotis sylvatica*												
Foxglove / *Digitalis "Foxy"*												
Hollyhock / *Alcea rosea*												
Johnny-Jump-Up / *Viola tricolor*												

Everlastings

Flowers that retain their form and color when dried are called "Everlastings."

Knowing when to harvest everlasting flowers is most important. Picking them too early or too late may cause them to darken as they dry or to become misshapen.

A gardener learns through experience when each type of flower is best for picking.

Flowers or foliage to be dried should be picked in the morning after the dew has dried and when the blooms are only partially open. Blooms continue to open as they dry. Pick only the most perfect flowers. Insect damage and poor shapes are more obvious after drying.

Hang Upside Down

Acroclinum
Bells of Ireland
Celosia
Craspedia
Globe Amaranth
Hair's Tail Grass
Hydrangea
Larkspur
Rose, Century II
Salvia leucantha
Salvia, "Victoria"
Statice, florist
Statice suworowii
Strawflower
Tansy
Xeranthemum
Yarrow

Hang Right-Side Up Through Hardware Cloth

Chives
Queen Anne's Lace

Bloom Chart For Cool Season Annuals

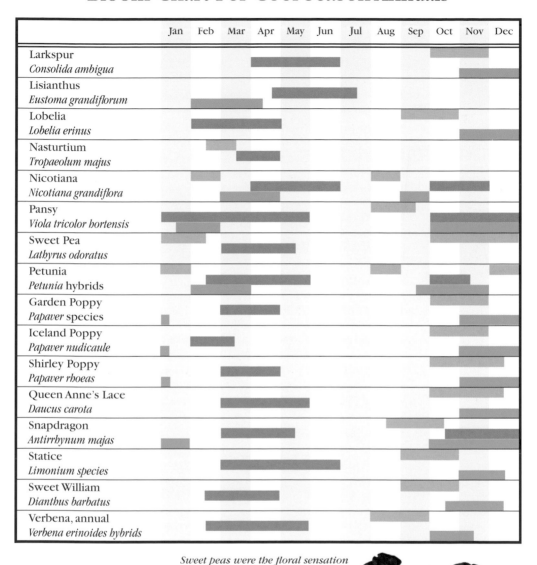

= Seed
= Bloom
= Transplant

Sweet peas were the floral sensation of the late Victorian era and have been a popular annual ever since. They can be grown as shrubby plants, climbing onto tripods or along a fence. Sweet pea vines will attach themselves to most any type of support. Planted in vegetable gardens they attract bees and other pollinators. Sweet peas should be directly seeded and seeds can be nicked or soaked in water for several hours to soften the seed coating. Using these colorful and fragrant flowers gives a cottage feel to a garden.

Bloom Chart For Perennials

	Jan	Feb	Mar	Apr	May	Jun	Jul	Aug	Sep	Oct	Nov	Dec
Angel Trumpet *Datura species*						■	■	■	■	■		
Hardy Begonia *Begonia grandis*					■	■	■	■	■	■		
Butterflyweed *Asclepias species*						■	■	■	■	■	■	
Chrysanthemum *Chrysanthemum*			■							■	■	■
"Cashmere Bouquet" *Clerodendrum*					■	■	■	■	■			
Coreopsis *Coreopsis grandiflora*				■	■	■	■					
Daylily *Hemerocallis hybrids*					■	■	■					
Echinacea *Echinacea purpurea*					■	■	■	■	■	■	■	
Four O'clock *Mirabilis jalapa*					■	■	■	■	■	■	■	
Gaillardia *Gaillardia grandiflora*				■	■	■	■	■	■	■	■	
Gerbera Daisy *Gerbera jamesonii*		■	■	■	■	■	■	■	■	■	■	■
Native Hibiscus *Hibiscus moscheutos*			■	■	■	■	■	■	■			
Jacobinia *Jacobinia camea*					■	■	■	■	■	■	■	
Jewels Of Opar *Talinum paniculatum*					■	■	■	■	■	■		
Hosta *Hosta species*				■	■	■						
Lantana *Lantana camara & others*					■	■	■	■	■	■	■	
Liriope *Liriope muscari*						■	■					
Loosestrife *Lythrum salicaria*						■	■					

Lantana grows well in full sunlight and summer heat and is a favorite of butterflies.

■ = Seed
■ = Bloom

Bloom Chart For Perennials

	Jan	Feb	Mar	Apr	May	Jun	Jul	Aug	Sep	Oct	Nov	Dec
Summer Phlox *Phlox paniculata*					■	■	■	■				
Louisiana Phlox *Phlox divaricata*			■									
Physostegia *Physostegia virginiana*							■	■				
Plumbago *Plumbago auriculata*					■	■	■	■	■	■		
Rudbeckia *Rudbeckia hirta hybrids*				■	■	■	■		■	■		
Mexican Sage *Salvia leucantha*									■	■	■	
Blue Salvia, "Victoria" *Salvia farinacea*				■	■	■	■	■	■	■		
Salvia guarinatica					■	■	■	■	■	■	■	
Shasta Daisy *Chrysanthemum x superbum*				■	■							
Stokesia *Stokesia laevis*				■	■	■	■					
Verbena *Verbena rigida & others*				■	■	■	■					
Veronica *Veronica species*				■	■							
Woods Violet *Viola odorata*	■	■	■									■

The Versatile Blossom

Dry flowers to use in sachets and aromatherapy projects.

Bake edible flowers such as roses and calendula into cakes, breads and cookies.

Press flowers for personalized note cards.

Add flowers to herbal vinegars.

Preserve edible flowers (viola, pansies) in sugar and use to decorate cakes.

Garnish with edible flowers.

Partial List of Edible Flowers

Anise Hyssop	Lilac
Arugula	Marigold
Basil	Mint
Bachelor's Button	Nasturtium
Bee Balm	Okra
Broccoli	Pansy
Calendula	Pineapple Sage
Chervil	Rose
Chicory	Rosemary
Chrysanthemum	Sage
Dandelion	Scarlet Runner Bean
Dianthus	Scented Geraniums
Dill	Snapdragon
Elderberry	Squash
English Daisy	Sunflower
Fennel	Thyme
Hibiscus	Tulip
Hollyhock	Violet

Bloom Chart For Bulbs And Related Plants

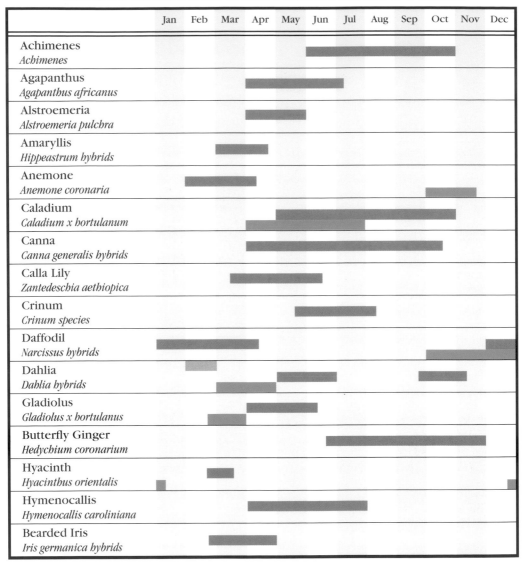

	Jan	Feb	Mar	Apr	May	Jun	Jul	Aug	Sep	Oct	Nov	Dec
Achimenes *Achimenes*						████	████	████	████	████		
Agapanthus *Agapanthus africanus*				████	████	████						
Alstroemeria *Alstroemeria pulchra*				████								
Amaryllis *Hippeastrum hybrids*			████									
Anemone *Anemone coronaria*		████								████		
Caladium *Caladium x hortulanum*				████	████	████	████	████	████			
Canna *Canna generalis hybrids*				████	████	████	████	████	████			
Calla Lily *Zantedeschia aethiopica*				████	████							
Crinum *Crinum species*						████	████					
Daffodil *Narcissus hybrids*		████	████							████	████	██
Dahlia *Dahlia hybrids*		██		████	████	████				████		
Gladiolus *Gladiolus x hortulanus*			████	████	████							
Butterfly Ginger *Hedychium coronarium*							████	████	████	████		
Hyacinth *Hyacinthus orientalis*	██		████									██
Hymenocallis *Hymenocallis caroliniana*				████	████	████						
Bearded Iris *Iris germanica hybrids*			████	████								

Bulbs 101
by Greg Grant

Bulb: A herbaceous plant with a fleshy underground storage organ made up of modified leaves. Includes both annual and perennial types. *Examples:* daffodils, amaryllis, and lilies. Often loosely includes other types of storage organs including tubers (caladiums), corms (gladiolus), rhizomes (iris), tuberous roots (daylilies), etc.

Annual bulb: A bulbous plant that is only useful for one season (doesn't reliably return and bloom each year). *Examples:* tulips, Dutch hyacinths, and caladiums.

Short-lived bulb: A bulbous plant that only performs well for a few years and gradually declines. *Examples:* large flowered daffodils, most true lilies, and most gladiolus.

Spring bulb: Bulbs that bloom in late winter or early spring. Most of these grow foliage during the winter and spring and go dormant in

Bloom Chart For Bulbs And Related Plants

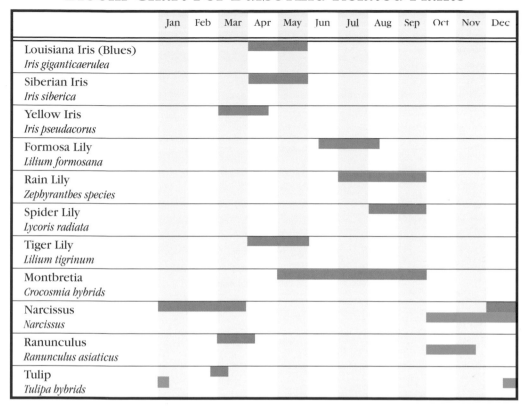

	Jan	Feb	Mar	Apr	May	Jun	Jul	Aug	Sep	Oct	Nov	Dec
Louisiana Iris (Blues) *Iris giganticaerulea*				▓	▓							
Siberian Iris *Iris siberica*				▓								
Yellow Iris *Iris pseudacorus*			▓									
Formosa Lily *Lilium formosana*							▓	▓				
Rain Lily *Zephyranthes species*								▓	▓	▓		
Spider Lily *Lycoris radiata*									▓	▓		
Tiger Lily *Lilium tigrinum*					▓							
Montbretia *Crocosmia hybrids*						▓	▓	▓	▓			
Narcissus *Narcissus*	▓	▓	▓								▓	▓
Ranunculus *Ranunculus asiaticus*			▓								▓	
Tulip *Tulipa hybrids*	▓		▓									▓

the summer. *Examples:* jonquils, snowflakes, and narcissus.

Summer bulb: Bulbs that grow and bloom during the late spring and summer. Most are tropical in origin, go dormant during the winter, and are somewhat tender and grown primarily outdoors only in the South. *Examples:* crinums, hymenocallis, and cannas.

Fall bulb: Bulbs that bloom in late summer and fall after a summer drought-induced dormancy. They normally bloom without foliage and grow foliage during the fall and winter. *Examples:* spider lily (*Lycoris*), oxblood lily, and rain lilies.

Naturalize: Bulbs multiply and spread on their own and seemingly grow "wild."

Perennialize: Bulbs return each year as perennials but may or may not naturalize.

Characteristics of bulbs: Easy, low maintenance, drought tolerant, light feeders, more expensive, long lived, mostly propagated by division.

Soil requirements: Not particular. Good drainage is best for most. Annual types require "annual soil mix."

▓	= Seed
▓	= Bloom
▓	= Transplant

Bloom Chart For Shrubs

	Jan	Feb	Mar	Apr	May	Jun	Jul	Aug	Sep	Oct	Nov	Dec
Abutilon *Abutilon pictum hybrids*	■	■	■	■	■	■	■	■	■	■	■	■
Althea *Hibiscus syriacus*						■	■	■	■			
Azalea *Rhododendron hybrids*			■	■						■	■	
Butterfly Bush *Buddleia alternifolia*					■	■	■					
Camellia *Camellia japonica*	■	■	■									■
Camellia, Sasanqua *Camellia sasanqua*										■	■	■
Forsythia *Forsythia intermedia*		■										
Gardenia *Gardenia jasminoides*					■	■						
Indian Hawthorne *Raphiolepsis indica*				■	■							
Holly, berries *Ilex species*	■	■	■							■	■	■
Winter Honeysuckle *Lonicera fragrantissima*	■	■										■
Hydrangea *Hydrangea macrophylla*					■	■	■					
Oakleaf Hydrangea *Hydrangea quercifolia*					■	■						

Because of the many colors, bloom seasons, size and form, azaleas may be placed as focal points in a landscape, grouped around trees, used as hedges or screens, or planted in beds or containers.

Azaleas are easy to grow and are usually free of pests. To successfully grow these beautiful plants, the following guidelines for care will make the job easier:

Plant in partial shade with a slightly acid soil, use a mulch of pine bark or pine needles, and provide good drainage but moist roots. Pruning should be done soon after blooming. If petal blight becomes a problem, it can be controlled with a fungicidal spray in the spring.

■ = Bloom

Bloom Chart For Shrubs

	Jan	Feb	Mar	Apr	May	Jun	Jul	Aug	Sep	Oct	Nov	Dec
Primrose Jasmine *Jasmine mesnyi*		██	██									
Ligustrum *Ligustrum japonicum*				██	██							
Mock Orange *Philadelphus coronarius*				██	██							
Oleander *Nerium oleander*						██	██	██	██			
Pittosporum *Pittosporum tobira*			██									
Pyracantha *Pyracantha coccinea*	█										██	██
Flowering Quince *Chaenomeles speciosa*	██	██	██									
Roses *Rosa hybrids*				██	██	██	██	██	██	██		
Bridalwreath Spirea *Spirea cantoniensis*			██	██								
Popcorn Spirea *Spirea prunifolia*		██	██									
Yaupon Holly, berries *Ilex vomitoria*	█										██	██

Recommended Azaleas

To extend the flowering season, add early (Red Ruffle) and late (Macrantha) blooming azaleas. Coordinate hues and try not to use more than 3 or 4 colors or the yard may look cluttered. Most azaleas fall in either purple/pink shades or orange/coral shades. These two groups do not mix easily.

Reliable azalea varieties include:

Daphne Salmon - compact, salmon pink
Fielder's White - spreading growth, white
Southern Charm - large, rosy-pink flower
Formosa - tall, purple
Judge Solomon/Pink Formosa - tall, lavender-pink
Pride of Mobile - tall, rose-pink
Red Formosa - deep cranberry
President Clay - tall, salmon

G.G. Gerbing/King's White - medium height, white
George Taber - medium height, white with lavender blotch, looks pale lavender
Fashion - medium height, light salmon, repeating bloom in fall
Macrantha - sporadic late-bloomer, coral-pink
Red Ruffle - early dwarf, double deep red, beautiful in mass
Pink Ruffle - medium, double pink
Wakabisu - late dwarf, peach

There are many other varieties that are just as beautiful. A good rule to remember when choosing is that the smaller the leaves, the more temperamental the plant. The tiny-leaved varieties demand shade, perfect drainage, a large amount of organic matter and are less forgiving of water stresses.

Bloom Chart For Trees

	Jan	Feb	Mar	Apr	May	Jun	Jul	Aug	Sep	Oct	Nov	Dec
Taiwan Cherry *Prunus campanulata*	■	■										
Crabapple *Malus species*			■	■								
Crape Myrtle *Lagerstroemia indica*						■	■	■				
Dogwood *Comus florida*			■	■								
Fringetree *Chionanthus virginicus*			■									
Japanese Magnolia *Magnolia x soulangiana*		■										
Southern Magnolia *Magnolia grandiflora*					■	■	■	■				
Flowering Pear *Pyrus calleryana*			■									
Redbud *Cercis Canadensis*		■	■									
Sweet Olive *Osmanthus fragrans*	■	■	■							■	■	■
Vitex *Vitex agnus-castus*					■	■						

The crape myrtle, a woody perennial, is one of the most versatile plants that can be grown in a garden. Crape myrtles can be grown in a variety of climates and range from 40-foot trees to 8-inch miniatures.

Most flowers are a result of growth from the previous year. The crape myrtle is quite different in that the flowers bloom on "new wood" or "new growth." Once the plant leafs out in the spring, frequent watering and fertilizer once a week or every two weeks will produce more flowers for a longer period of time.

Contrary to popular belief heavy pruning is not necessary for abundant flowering and often destroys the natural grace of the tree. Prune selectively and remove any suckers that may form.

Bloom Chart For Vines

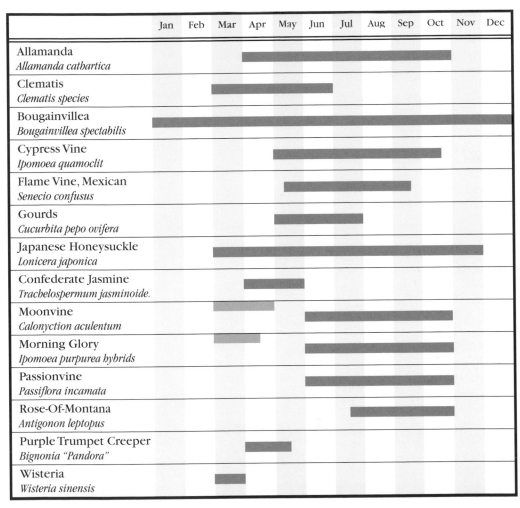

	Jan	Feb	Mar	Apr	May	Jun	Jul	Aug	Sep	Oct	Nov	Dec
Allamanda *Allamanda cathartica*					Bloom	Bloom	Bloom	Bloom	Bloom	Bloom		
Clematis *Clematis species*			Bloom	Bloom	Bloom	Bloom						
Bougainvillea *Bougainvillea spectabilis*	Bloom	Bloom	Bloom	Bloom	Bloom	Bloom	Bloom	Bloom	Bloom	Bloom	Bloom	Bloom
Cypress Vine *Ipomoea quamoclit*					Bloom	Bloom	Bloom	Bloom	Bloom	Bloom		
Flame Vine, Mexican *Senecio confusus*					Bloom	Bloom	Bloom	Bloom				
Gourds *Cucurbita pepo ovifera*					Bloom	Bloom	Bloom					
Japanese Honeysuckle *Lonicera japonica*				Bloom	Bloom	Bloom	Bloom	Bloom	Bloom	Bloom	Bloom	Bloom
Confederate Jasmine *Trachelospermum jasminoide.*				Bloom	Bloom							
Moonvine *Calonyction aculentum*			Seed	Seed		Bloom	Bloom	Bloom	Bloom	Bloom		
Morning Glory *Ipomoea purpurea hybrids*			Seed	Seed		Bloom	Bloom	Bloom	Bloom	Bloom		
Passionvine *Passiflora incamata*						Bloom	Bloom	Bloom	Bloom	Bloom		
Rose-Of-Montana *Antigonon leptopus*								Bloom	Bloom	Bloom		
Purple Trumpet Creeper *Bignonia "Pandora"*				Bloom	Bloom							
Wisteria *Wisteria sinensis*			Bloom									

= Seed
= Bloom

The Rose of Montana vine grows well in the South. It may freeze back in the winter but will return in the spring producing an abundance of flowers in the late summer and fall.

Harvest Chart

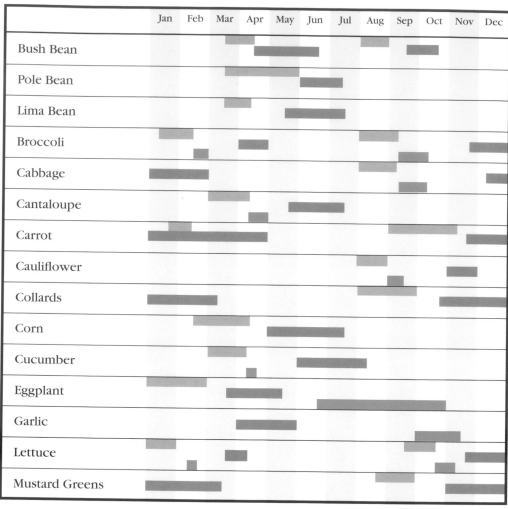

	Jan	Feb	Mar	Apr	May	Jun	Jul	Aug	Sep	Oct	Nov	Dec
Bush Bean												
Pole Bean												
Lima Bean												
Broccoli												
Cabbage												
Cantaloupe												
Carrot												
Cauliflower												
Collards												
Corn												
Cucumber												
Eggplant												
Garlic												
Lettuce												
Mustard Greens												

= Seed
= Harvest
= Transplant

Harvest Chart

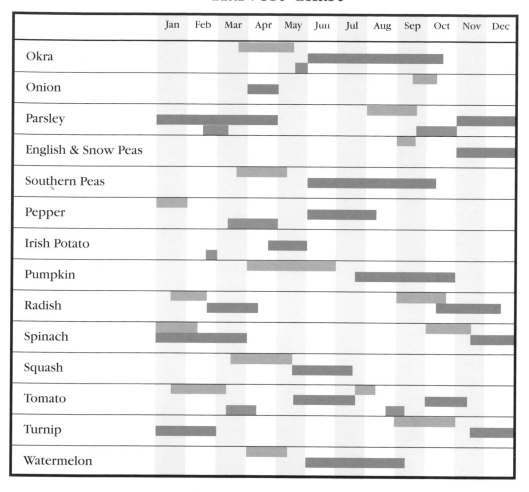

Yellow squash bloom throughout the summer in the kitchen garden at Magnolia Mound Plantation. Squash blossoms are edible both raw and cooked.

There is a recent trend in rose gardening that shows a move away from traditional grandifloras and hybrid teas. Gardeners now are more interested in old garden roses and landscape/shrub roses that are easier to care for and fit well into the landscape. The following recommended plants are only a partial list of available roses.

OLD GARDEN ROSES

China Roses - Flowers are produced constantly. The growth is bushy and twiggy, fits well into landscapes and thrives in heavy clay soils.

Archduke Charles, *red blend*

Cramoisi superieur, *red*

Ducher, *white*

Louis Philippe, *light red*

Martha Gonzales, *red*

Mutabilis, *flowers change from yellow to pink*

Old Blush, *pink*

Green Rose, *green*

Tea Roses - Flowers are large and everblooming. Bushes are robust and disease resistant. This group of roses was used to develop hybrid teas.

Bon Silene, *dark pink*

Duchesse de Brabant, *light pink*

Mrs. B. R. Cant, *red*

Mrs. Dudley Cross, *yellow blend*

Sombreuil, *white climber*

Noisette Roses - Everblooming well-behaved climbers, the flowers are fragrant and grow in clusters that hang down from the canes.

Champney's Pink Cluster, *light pink*

Lamarque, *white*

Alfred Carriere, *white*

Natchitoches Noisette, *light pink*

Reve d'Or, *pale gold*

Souvenir de la Malmaison is a favorite Bourbon rose for many Southern gardeners.

Bourbon Roses - Produce very fragrant flowers on everblooming robust shrubs or climbers but are more susceptible to black spot than other old garden roses.

Maggie, *red*

Souvenir de la Malmaison, *pink*

Zephirine Drouhin, *pink*

Boule de Neige, *white*

Mme. Isaac Pereire, *dark pink*

FLORIBUNDA

This bush type plant may be used for hedges with continuous blooming flowers born in clusters.

Betty Prior, *single, dark-pink*

Europeana, *brilliant-red*

Simplicity, *pink*

Summer Snow, *dwarf, white*

HYBRID TEAS

Flowers are born singly on large stems or in small clusters and continuously bloom.

Cecile Bruner, *old pink sweetheart*

Century II, *pink*

Chrysler Imperial, *dark red*

Double Delight, *red and white bicolor*

First prize, *pink blend*

Miss All American Beauty, *medium pink*

Mr. Lincoln, *dark red*

Oregold, *dark yellow*

Peace, *yellow and pink blend*

Pristine, *pale pink*

Queen Elizabeth, *soft pink*

Tiffany, *pink blend*

Tropicana, *orange-red*

Recommended Fruits

If choosing a fruit not listed, make sure the chilling requirement is between 500 and 650 hours.

APPLE

Molly Delicious

BLUEBERRY

Tifblue, Powder Blue, Climax, Premier, Brightwell

BRAMBLES

Boysenberry, Youngberry, Brison, Womack, Brazos, Cheyenne, Shawnee, Roseborough, Kiowa, Arapaha, Ouachita

RASPBERRIES

Dorman Red

CITRUS

Satsuma

Armstrong Early, Owari, Louisiana Early, Kimbrough, Early St. Anne, Brown's Select

Sweet Orange

Hamlin Sweet, Louisiana Sweet, Ambersweet, Moro Blood, Plaquemines, Pineapple Sweet, Valencia

Navel Orange

Washington

Grapefruit

Duncan, Rio Red, Ruby Red

Tangelo

Roland

Muscadine grapes, native to the southern United States, were first noted by North Carolina colonists in 1554.

Manderin

Ponkan

Lemon

Meyer

Tangerine

Dancy, Robinson, Sunburst, Orlando

Kumquat

Nagami, Meiwa

Fig

LSU Purple, LSU Gold, Celeste, O'Rourke, Champagne, Southeastern Brown Turkey, Alma, Tiger,

GRAPE

Bunch

Blue Lake, Conquistador, Miss Blanc, Miss Blue, Mid South, Suwanee

Mayhaw

Red Majesty, Royalty, Texas Star, Royal Star, Spectacular, Texas Super Berry

Muscadine

Carlos, Cowart, Nesbit, Granny Val, Tara, Ison

LOQUAT

Big Jim

NECTARINE

Armking, Sunred

PEACH

Florida King, LaFestival, Florida Gold Gulf Crest, Gulf Prince, Delta, Gulf King, Sam Houston, Florida Prince, Earli Grande, Texstar, Sun Grande

PEAR

Baldwin, Spalding, Orient

JAPANESE PERSIMMON

Tanenashi, Eureka, Fuyu, Fuyu Imoto, Hana Fuyu, Suruga

PINEAPPLE GUAVA

Coolidge, Triump

PLUM

Bruce, Byron Gold

STRAWBERRY

Chandler, Strawberry festival, Camarosa, Earliglow

Rescuing History

(Above) A watercolor sketch of Baton Rouge, Louisiana, painted by W.T. Kummer in 1821; from the Magnolia Mound Plantation archives at LSU Hill Memorial Library, Baton Rouge.

(Left) Interpreter Lynette Dutsch looks out the window of the children's bedroom at Magnolia Mound Plantation.

ON A HIGH RIDGE along the Mississippi River sits Magnolia Mound Plantation, one of the few surviving French plantation houses in the Baton Rouge region. Originally a four-room cottage, it was built in the 1790s by John Joyce, an Irish immigrant who had purchased the property from James Hillin. Joyce was married to Constance Rochon. The couple lived in Mobile rather than at Magnolia Mound, leaving the indigo plantation to be supervised by an overseer. Joyce was a merchant and builder and had many business ventures on the Gulf Coast.

In 1798 Constance was left a wealthy widow with two children when John Joyce drowned during a river trip. She married Armand Duplantier four years later. Duplantier owned a plantation across the river from Magnolia Mound and was himself a widower with four children. A native Frenchman, he served under the Marquis de Lafayette during the American Revolution and was a prominent local citizen. They subsequently moved to Magnolia Mound and with Constance's inheritance began improving the house. To satisfy his tastes that had been cultivated in France, Armand imported silks and wallpapers and updated the main rooms in the fashionable Federal style. He also added a cove ceiling to the parlor and embellished both the parlor and the dining room with moldings, paneling and carved mantelpieces. A rear gallery and several rooms were also added as their family grew to include five more children.

Historic Cemeteries in the South

There are many intimate, charming, historic cemeteries that dot the southern landscape. Many of them, forgotten by time, are now only a jumble of old stones and twisted vines.

The early 19th-century Highland Cemetery in Baton Rouge, Louisiana, was lost in a deep thicket until a few decades ago when someone cut a narrow path through the limbs and shrubs to find a beautiful historic treasure. The burial site was restored by 1978, revealing beautiful old tombs and names from the past.

The cemetery site was on a plantation first owned by George Garig, a German settler from Maryland. The Garig family and other highlanders (families who settled on the high ground along the Mississippi River) were buried there prior to 1813. In 1819 he deeded the burial site to the Catholic Congregation in Baton Rouge and it became the official cemetery of the families of the highlands. Other plantation owners also added land to the site.

Several members of the Duplantier family, of Magnolia Mound Plantation, are buried in Historic Highland Cemetery. Most importantly is Armand Duplantier, who was laid to rest in the old Highland Cemetery with military honors in 1827.

The Historic Highland Cemetery is located approximately 1.5 miles southeast of Magnolia Mound Plantation on Oxford Avenue, near the south gates of Louisiana State University and is open to the public.

The overseer's house at Magnolia Mound is original to the plantation, circa 1870.

Constance and Armand traveled down river to New Orleans to purchase their furniture. The shops in New Orleans, a major port even at that time, offered European furniture, fashionable mahogany neo-classical furniture that was popular on the East coast, and locally made furnishings of cherry, walnut and cypress. When Magnolia Mound had been completely decorated it was as elegant as any house built along the Mississippi River. The current interpretation of the house museum is based on the years that it was owned by the Duplantier family from 1802 to 1830.

The Duplantier family raised cotton and later sugar cane on the 900-acre plantation and was prosperous in the begin-

Magnolia Mound Plantation, a fine example of the architectural influences of early settlers from France and the West Indies, is one of the earliest buildings built in Baton Rouge and its most historically significant 18th-century structure.

Magnolia Mound Plantation in a deteriorated state, circa 1928.

ning. After about 1814 their fortunes began to change. The couple eventually sold off various holdings and by 1827 Armand had died leaving Magnolia Mound Plantation as the last property of the family's once affluent life.

The ownership of the property passed through several families. By the 1960s the house was empty, in great need of repair and threatened with demolition. Preservationists, led by the Foundation for Historical Louisiana, spearheaded the restoration efforts. The Baton Rouge Recreation and Parks Commission purchased the property in 1966 and by 1975 the House was opened to the public. The Friends of Magnolia Mound Plantation owns the exquisite collection of furniture, decorative items and artifacts that are displayed at the plantation.

Magnolia Mound Plantation interpreter, Eunice Pavageau, demonstrates the sparse interior of a typical plantation slave cabin.

The Other Side of Plantation Life

THE MISSION OF Magnolia Mound Plantation is not just to show how plantation owners and their families lived during the 18th- and 19th-centuries, but to present how slaves lived from day to day during this tumultuous time in American history.

The "other side of plantation life" is demonstrated in programming developed as a dramatic presentation offered each year during Black History Month. *In Their Own Voices: American Slaves Tell Their Story* is based on extensive research of *Slave Narratives from the Federal Writers' Project, 1926-1938*, a collection of over 2,300 first-person accounts of slavery and the respondents' own reactions to bondage. This Works Progress Administration collection of

oral histories stands as one of the most enduring and noteworthy achievements of the WPA. Other important collections used were found in the Louisiana State Archives, The Louisiana State Library and the Archives Department of the John Brother Cade Library at Southern University. A concert of Negro spirituals and contemporary music by African American composers is also included in the programming. By providing dialog in a public venue through this programming, people from all walks of life are able to hear the words of slaves and feel the sorrow, laughter, triumph and pain of those who suffered.

At one time Magnolia Mound Plantation had slave quarters consisting of 16 cabins with 50 slaves. Visitors are able to experience a closer look at the home life of enslaved men, women and children. Inside the cabin is a poignant setting of a slave family's sparsely furnished one-room abode. An interactive exhibit, entitled "A Peculiar Institution: An Exhibit of Slavery in the South," includes captivating songs of the slaves and pictures and artifacts that depict the journey of slaves from Africa, their lives on the plantation and their dreams of freedom. Plantation documents list the names of many of the slaves and their family members who worked the fields of tobacco, indigo, sugar cane and cotton.

Students who visit the plantation as a part of a school trip have the opportunity to take part in a program entitled "A Day in the Life of a Slave." In addition to studying the exhibit in the slave cabin, the students learn why slavery existed in America, about the economic history of the region and what daily hardships slaves endured on the plantation. A variety of daily chores are assigned to participating students who then take part in doing only some of the jobs that slaves did every day, such as laundry, grinding corn, deseeding and carding cotton, making bousillage, feeding poultry and gathering wood.

Through these programs, Magnolia Mound strives to shed light on this often ignored aspect of Southern plantation history. With research projects under way and constant investigation of cutting edge scholarly publications, Magnolia Mound Plantation is proud to dedicate resources to the body of knowledge surrounding slave life.

An 1830s slave cabin, originally part of the Cherie Quarters on Riverlake Plantation, was relocated to Magnolia Mound in the mid-1990s.

HISTORIC NOTE

Mocha Ware

One of the earliest mentions of Mocha ware was in the Boston Daily Advertiser in 1815 listing pieces of various designs for sale. Mocha ware or dipped ware is actually creamware that has been decorated with dipped brush patterns on backgrounds of tan, terra cotta or blue. Mocha ware, though hard to find, has recently become a popular collectors' item.

Shards of Mocha ware have been found during archaeological digs on the grounds of Magnolia Mound Plantation and include the cable (earthworm), three color cat's eye, dendritic (seaweed and trees), Enoch wood and various rouletted and combed designs. Reproduction Mocha ware mugs are on display in the kitchen.

Historic Kitchen and Garden

IN EARLY SOUTHERN plantation houses, the kitchen was often the heart of the home, even though it may have been completely separate from the main house.

It was usually a small wooden or brick structure that was built away from the house because of the danger of fire and the intense heat that was generated while cooking. This also reduced cooking odors and noise from the kitchen workers. The major problem with this arrangement was the transportation of food from the kitchen to the main house, especially during rainy seasons.

Open-hearth cookery in a fireplace required much preparation before the cooking actually began. Supplying only one hearth took a large amount of wood. Achieving a good bed of coals could take about an hour before small beds of coals could be raked onto the hearth or arranged in the fireplace for food items to be cooked at a variety of temperatures. Preparing the bake oven was a more complicated and longer process. Cooking in an open hearth was a dangerous job for the women of yesteryear. Catching fire during cooking was a common problem and the cause of many deaths. Cooks working in demonstration plantation kitchens of today wear only cotton clothing, keep blankets on hand to smother fires and have pails of water ready at all times.

Open-hearth cookery has become a subject of public interest. Cooking in this manner is a challenge, a pleasure and a fascinating link with earlier times.

The reproduction of a working kitchen of the early 1800s was completed in 1979 at Magnolia Mound Plantation. This addition augments the educational goals in depicting the culture, foodways and lifestyle of this period. Research in historical records, visits to other kitchens of the same period and use of old materials all contribute to its authentic appearance. Regular open-hearth cooking demonstrations, using recipes of the period and authentic cookware and methods, add life and color to the interpretive program.

HISTORIC NOTE

Grenouilles en Fricassee de Poulet

The frog should have legs of a good size to cut from the body. Cut the feet off, then skin the legs. Put them in boiling water then remove them to fresh water, and put them in a casserole with some mushrooms, a bouquet of parsley and chives, a clove of garlic, two cloves of clove, a piece of butter. Place it on the fire with these seasonings; add a pinch of flour, moisten with a glass of white wine and a little bouillon, put salt, lots of pepper, cook and reduce the gravy, thicken with yolks of three eggs, a piece of butter and then throw in a little minced parsley.

Tante Huppe

From *The Magnolia Mound Plantation Kitchen Book, Being a Compendium of Foodways and Customs of Early Louisiana 1795-1841*, Composed by Dedicated Friends of Magnolia Mound Plantation, Magnolia Mound Plantation House, 1986, p.29.

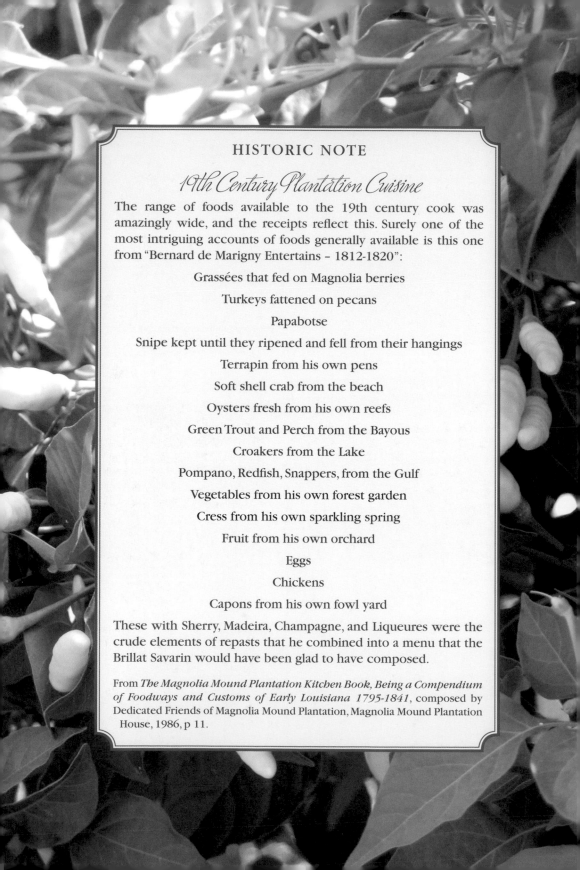

HISTORIC NOTE

19th Century Plantation Cuisine

The range of foods available to the 19th century cook was amazingly wide, and the receipts reflect this. Surely one of the most intriguing accounts of foods generally available is this one from "Bernard de Marigny Entertains – 1812-1820":

Grassées that fed on Magnolia berries

Turkeys fattened on pecans

Papabotse

Snipe kept until they ripened and fell from their hangings

Terrapin from his own pens

Soft shell crab from the beach

Oysters fresh from his own reefs

Green Trout and Perch from the Bayous

Croakers from the Lake

Pompano, Redfish, Snappers, from the Gulf

Vegetables from his own forest garden

Cress from his own sparkling spring

Fruit from his own orchard

Eggs

Chickens

Capons from his own fowl yard

These with Sherry, Madeira, Champagne, and Liqueures were the crude elements of repasts that he combined into a menu that the Brillat Savarin would have been glad to have composed.

From *The Magnolia Mound Plantation Kitchen Book, Being a Compendium of Foodways and Customs of Early Louisiana 1795-1841*, composed by Dedicated Friends of Magnolia Mound Plantation, Magnolia Mound Plantation House, 1986, p 11.

Soon after the kitchen restoration was completed, research began on planning and installing an historic kitchen garden, as it was an important part of the economy of a plantation. Vegetables, fruit and herbs were grown for everyday use for the inhabitants of a plantation. After visiting many existing historic gardens across the country and consulting with experts in the field, a plan was designed that would represent a typical kitchen garden that may have been seen on the plantation during the early 1800s. The garden is now included in educational tours and produce from the garden is used in the preparation of cooking demonstrations.

Popular Plants in Nineteenth-Century Kitchen Gardens

Artichokes
Asparagus
Beans
Beets
Bloodwort
Broccoli
Bredes or False
   Spinach
Cabbage
Carrots
Cauliflower
Celery
Chervil
Chives
Cucumber
Eggplant

Endive
Escarole
Garden Cress
Garlic
Goosefoot
Gourds
Green Onions
Jerusalem
   Artichokes
Kidney Beans
Lamb's Lettuce
Leeks
Lentils
Lettuce
Melons
Mushrooms

Mustard
Onions
Parsley
Parsnips
Peanuts
Peas
Peppers
Pole Beans
Potatoes
Pumpkins
Radishes
Salsify
Scallions
Scorzonera (Black
   Salsify)
Shallots

Sorrel
Spinach
Squash
Strawberries
Sweet Potatoes
Tomato
Turnips
Watercress
Wild Rocket

From Jacques-Felix Lelievre's New Louisiana Gardener translated by Sally Kittredge Reeves, LSU Press, 2001, pp. 76-80; 81-104.

Magnolia Mound Plantation

2161 Nicholson Drive
Baton Rouge, LA 70802

(between downtown and the Louisiana State University campus)

(225) 343-4955

Magnolia Mound Plantation is a rare survivor of the vernacular architecture influenced by early settlers from France and the West Indies. This venerable landmark is unique in southern Louisiana not simply because of its age, quality of restoration or outstanding collection, but because it is still a vital part of the community. Through educational programs, workshops, lectures, festivals and other special events, Magnolia Mound illustrates and interprets the lifestyle of the French Creoles who formed the fascinating culture which still influences and pervades life in southern Louisiana.

Located on 14 acres of the original 900 that once made up Magnolia Mound, the plantation offers a unique opportunity to learn about a working plantation from the early 1800s.

PLACES TO EXPLORE INCLUDE:

Historic House Museum: Magnolia Mound Plantation is accredited by the American Association of Museums and is listed on the National Register of Historic Places. The museum is open to the public daily with trained interpreters in period costumes conducting tours.

Open-Hearth Kitchen: The reconstructed separate outdoor kitchen is authentically furnished with vintage utensils such as spider pots, sugar nippers, waffle iron, olla jar and reflector ovens. Cooking demonstrations are held in the cooler months.

Overseer's House: The overseer's house is original to the plantation, c. 1870, and was home to the man hired to run the day-to-day operations of the plantation.

Quarter House: A double slave cabin, c. 1830, has one living quarter furnished appropriately to the period. The adjoining room contains an exhibit of slave life on a Louisiana plantation. The slave cabin was moved from Riverlake Plantation.

Pigeonnier: The pigeonnier, c. 1825, was used to hold nesting boxes for house squab and various game birds.

Kitchen Garden: The kitchen garden is planted with vegetables, fruit and herbs that were grown in the 1800s.

Carriage House: A collection of vintage tools, as well as a weaver's workshop that depicts plantation chores c. 1800-1820 is on display.

Visitors' Center: Purchase gifts and informative books and enjoy ongoing exhibits.

MAGNOLIA MOUND HOURS

Monday - Saturday 10 a.m. - 4 p.m. and Sunday 1 p.m. - 4 p.m.
Tours begin on the hour from 10 a.m. until 3 p.m.
Admission is charged.

Visit www.brec.org for more information about Magnolia Mound Plantation.

Garden Notes

Garden Notes

Garden Notes

Garden Notes

Garden Notes

Garden Notes

Garden Notes

Garden Notes

Garden Notes

Garden Notes